JOURNAL FOR THE STUDY OF THE OLD TESTAMENT
SUPPLEMENT SERIES
153

Editors
David J.A. Clines
Philip R. Davies

JSOT Press
Sheffield

The Psalms and their Readers

Interpretive Strategies for Psalm 18

Donald K. Berry

Journal for the Study of the Old Testament
Supplement Series 153

BS
1450
18th
.B470
1993

Published by JSOT Press
JSOT Press is an imprint of
Sheffield Academic Press Ltd
343 Fulwood Road
Sheffield S10 3BP
England

Typeset by Sheffield Academic Press
and
Printed on acid-free paper in Great Britain
by Biddles Ltd
Guildford

British Library Cataloguing in Publication Data

Berry, Donald K.
    Psalms and Their Readers: Interpretive
    Strategies for Psalm 18.—(JSOT
    Supplement Series, ISSN 0309-0787; No. 153)
    I. Title II. Series
    223

    ISBN 1-85075-399-7

CONTENTS

LIST OF TABLES

ABBREVIATIONS

AB	Anchor Bible
ANE, I	J. Pritchard (ed.), *The Ancient Near East: An Anthology of Texts and Pictures*
ANE, II	J. Pritchard (ed.), *The Ancient Near East Volume 2: A New Anthology of Texts and Pictures*
BDB	F. Brown, S. Driver and C. Briggs, *A Hebrew and English Lexicon of the Old Testament*
BHK	R. Kittel (ed.), *Biblia hebraica*
BHS	K. Elliger and W. Rudolf (eds.), *Biblia hebraica stuttgartensia*
BJRL	*Bulletin of the John Rylands University Library of Manchester*
BKAT	Biblischer Kommentar: Altes Testament
CBQ	*Catholic Biblical Quarterly*
ICC	International Critical Commentary
JBL	*Journal of Biblical Literature*
JQR	*Jewish Quarterly Review*
JSOT	*Journal for the Study of the Old Testament*
RevExp	*Review and Expositor*
RSV	Revised Standard Version
SBLSP	*SBL Seminar Papers*
WBC	Word Biblical Commentary

Chapter 1

INTRODUCTION

Recent developments in biblical hermeneutics and criticism have largely focused on narrative and, to a lesser degree, prophecy. While literary methods and approaches abound in these areas, few comprehensive approaches to the Psalms and other Hebrew poetry have been suggested. In the past thirty-five years, only rhetorical criticism (and stylistics, a closely related discipline) has been introduced as a method of Psalms research. Form criticism, which reached its zenith with Gunkel at the turn of the century, laid the groundwork for rhetorical criticism. These two complementary methods are by far the dominant perspectives on Psalms interpretation.

While these two approaches continue to prove themselves productive, they cannot provide a matrix for the latest literary approach: reader-response criticism. Form criticism is fundamentally 'author'-centered, while rhetorical criticism focuses upon 'the text itself' as an aesthetic object. Neither provides for a 'reader-oriented' perspective.

This study offers a fresh angle on the Psalms by treating a representative psalm as a 'read' object. The thesis is that an analysis of Psalm 18 from a reader-oriented point of view can offer substantially new and productive insights on the psalm itself and Psalms study in general. This hypothesis is tested by means of four separate analyses of Psalm 18. First, a textual study establishes a reliable translation; secondly, a form-critical analysis presents a synopsis of research on Psalm 18 with some original contributions; thirdly, a rhetorical approach supplements the form-critical analysis by accentuating the unique features of Psalm 18 as an example of its *Gattung*; and fourthly, speech act theory and other reader-oriented strategies are employed to analyze the psalm against the background of language and discourse, with particular attention to the reader/hearer. To conclude the study, the findings of each analysis are weighed and compared. Some suggestions are offered concerning the value of each approach for future study, and the strengths and weaknesses of each, especially speech act criticism, are spelled out. The thesis will be affirmed if it is possible to demonstrate that significantly different avenues for interpretation are opened by the reader-oriented approach. The purposes of this study are threefold. The primary aim (and the simplest) is to provide a comprehensive analysis of Psalm 18. As a second concern, an overview of the various approaches is presented. Each section is introduced by a brief outline of the presuppositions and orientation of the method with emphasis upon the view of biblical literature assumed by each approach. The third, and most immediate, purpose is to introduce a contemporary literary perspective on the Psalms.

This perspective begins with the consideration of the psalm in question as a freestanding lyric poem. This appears a more radical departure from the studies of Robert Lowth and Hermann Gunkel than it actually is. Although these scholars apply their insights almost exclusively to Hebrew poetry, neither the study of parallel lines nor the study of forms is restricted to Hebrew texts. Both approaches employ accepted principles of literary interpretation which are developed in conjunction with a wide array of texts and subsequently adapted for application to Hebrew literature. For this reason, the designation 'lyric poetry' may be used without apprehensiveness regarding the application of contemporary notions to ancient texts. When biblical poetry is designated and interpreted as lyric poetry, the critic is merely bridging the gap between older, 'theologized' modes of study and newer modes which have not yet become institutions within biblical studies. Norman Gottwald attempts a similar synthesis on a wider scale in his recent introduction.[1]

When the Psalms are studied as lyric poetry, the opportunity arises for the application of many major literary approaches to the Psalms. In this connection, rhetorical analysis, reader-response criticism, and speech act theory will be highlighted. Rhetorical criticism is in part a more traditional approach, being linked with form criticism. But its emphasis on the text as a self-sufficient object of study severs its connection to the historical origins of form criticism. This is the

---

1. N.K. Gottwald, *The Hebrew Bible: A Socio-Literary Introduction* (Philadelphia: Fortress Press, 1985).

orientation of the New Critics[1], who seek to free texts from expressive, historical, and psychological ties with the author. While earlier approaches discuss literature in terms of its author's intentions, New Critics substitute the 'text itself' and denote the former approach 'the intentional fallacy'.

Terry Eagleton characterizes the history of interpretation as a three-staged process. The first stage, described as author-centered, includes romantic, expressive, and pragmatic theories of literature as well as source criticism and, to some degree, redaction criticism. Form criticism can also be considered author-centered in that it is concerned with the personal and communal origins of a document. The second stage of the history of interpretation is text-centered. Formalism and New Criticism are each text-centered in their own way. Correlates in the biblical field include rhetorical criticism and stylistics. The third and present stage, according to Eagleton, is reader-oriented. This is the perspective of structuralism, deconstruction, and various reader-response theories, all of which are used in conjunction with biblical texts, and more frequently within the past ten years.[2] A reader-response approach to biblical poetry has been chosen for this study, and is employed in Chapter 5. Overtly structuralist or deconstructionist modes have been avoided, as they tend to be obscure and too technical. Psalm 18 is examined as 'read' literature, a perspective from which the author is important only as the encoder of the text. The psalm is decoded with primary emphasis upon the contemporary context. Within this analysis, several important approaches play a part and they are discussed below.

The reader-response criticism of Wolfgang Iser provides some groundwork. Iser is influenced by the phenomenology of Husserl and secondarily by the literary theory of Roman Ingarden. Iser sees the text and the reader as partners in the enterprise of reading. The text contains the intentional acts of the author; yet this does not imply that an author's feelings or subjective experiences are contained in the text. Instead, as indicated by the phenomenologists' view of consciousness as intentional, the essence of a literary work is the object it 'intends'. Objects are constituted by thought, and this concept of reality elicits the technical meaning of the word 'intention'. To Iser, the text

1. Including C. Brooks, W.K. Wimsatt, Jr, R. Penn Warren and others.

2   T. Eagleton, *Literary Theory: An Introduction* (Minneapolis: University of Minnesota Press, 1983), p. 74.

determines the reader's responses, but it is full of gaps which leave meaning indeterminate. The reader's responsibility is to fill in those gaps, but the reader's task is regulated by the determinate aspects of the text. Even though a variety of readings is possible, certain readings may be judged inappropriate, since all interpretation is governed by the text's determinate features.[1]

The core of this study rests in matters relating to Austin's speech act theory which separates ordinary speech into three components. Every speaker performs a *locutionary* act (speaking a sentence which has sense and reference). A speaker also performs an *illocutionary* act (speaking with an intended force, for example, to educate or alert). A speaker may also perform a *perlocutionary* act (speaking that results in an effect, for example, cheering or depressing the hearer). These are the three basic ways in which all sentences are used.[2] Austin avoids the tendency to analyze speech acts as true or false, and the types listed above reflect this, but they are based on an earlier distinction between performative and constative utterances. A constative utterance is a statement that has historical reference (a truth statement), and a performative is a statement in which the speaker 'does' something. The 'I do' of the wedding ceremony is performative since by its repetition in the proper context the speaker performs an action: the saying of the vows constitutes marriage.[3] Austin expands this category so that all spoken language, even apparently 'factual' statements, becomes performative, resulting in the categorization which began this paragraph.

When speech act theory is applied to written discourse, literature must be compared to ordinary language in some way. Most speech act theorists contend that literary language functions in the same way that ordinary language does, but that the context of the speech acts has changed. While Austin considers literature as an aberration from ordinary speech acts, a later trend described speech acts in literature as 'pretended' performatives.[4] In writing a work of fiction, then, the

---

1. W. Iser, *The Act of Reading: A Theory of Aesthetic Response* (Baltimore: Johns Hopkins University Press, 1978), pp. 66-68, 84-85, 170-231.
2. J.L. Austin, *How to Do Things with Words* (ed. J.O. Urmson and M. Sbisa; Cambridge, MA: Harvard University Press, 1975), pp. 98-102.
3. *How to Do Things with Words*, p. 6.
4. J.R. Searle, *Expression and Meaning: Studies in the Theory of Speech Acts* (Cambridge: University of Cambridge Press, 1979), pp. 65-70.

author pretends certain performances. The relation of these pretended speech acts to the audible speech acts which they imitate is equivalent to the concept of literary work as mimesis. For Aristotle, art imitates reality; in this scheme, a work of fiction is an imitation of ordinary speech acts. From this perspective, the ever-present 'I' of the Psalms may be read as a device presuming the participation of each reader, rather than as a projection of the writer's own voice.

Such points of view on the Psalms provide a critical outlet for the analysis of the affective nature of the Psalms. Stanley Fish has developed an approach known as 'affective stylistics' according to which an informed reader can gauge the effect of words and passages of a reading. Fish's proposition that the text is created by the reader seems somewhat extreme. The idea is that a text does not exist until it is read, and no two readings are alike. He distinguishes the published text from its individual readings. Here, each reader creates a somewhat different text, with the printed volume existing only as potential.[1]

Fish's suggestions regarding reading conventions are much more pertinent to this study than his view of texts. Each text may be understood only in terms of the conventions which the reading community shares. The assumption that reading always takes place within an interpretive community plays a fundamental role in Childs's canonical approach to scripture.[2] However, where Childs discusses textual history and transmission, Fish is only concerned with contemporary readings.

Two further literary concepts contribute to this study. The first of these is voice, with an emphasis upon the differing voices within the text as perceived by the reader, rather than the perspective in relation to the author. The use of voice is a rhetorical tool of the writer, and changes of voice offer clues to the type of roles expected for passive readers of psalms or those employing psalms in other contexts. The interest in voice assumes the second literary concept, which has already been mentioned: rhetoric. Such rhetoric is kin to Muilenburg's rhetorical criticism only in its origins with Aristotle's use of the term.[3] What the interpreter is most interested in is the text's persuasiveness:

1. S. Fish, *Is There a Text in This Class? The Authority of Interpretive Communities* (Cambridge, MA: Harvard University Press, 1980), pp. 42-44.
2. Fish, *Is There a Text in This Class?*, p. 14, and B. Childs, *Introduction to the Old Testament as Scripture* (Philadelphia: Fortress Press, 1979).
3. J. Muilenburg, 'Form Criticism and Beyond', *JBL* 88 (1969), pp.1-18.

how effective is the text, and how is that effect achieved? Identifying
the point of view of the 'implied author' is central.[1]

This study is a comparative one, describing its most original
contributions more fully than those of the traditional studies. With
respect to methodology, the textual, form-critical, and rhetorical
studies require only brief description, but the literary methodology
proposed is supplied with more extensive groundwork. Finally, the
method used for comparisons of the findings of these analyses requires
a brief outline.

Text criticism follows the standard practices, with precedence given
to the Masoretic Text. *BHS*[2] provides the framework and significant
variants are noted with brief explanations and succinct choices. In
determining the most desirable reading, (1) the semantics of the
passage are examined in light of its immediate context and its context
within the entire psalm, (2) the most difficult plausible reading is
preferred, (3) the shortest plausible reading is preferred, and (4) no
textual emendations are made on the basis of meter alone.

The tools employed in the textual study include the textual notes in
BHS and *BHK*.[3] The Septuagint is examined for evidence of alternative readings.[4] The parallel psalm, 2 Samuel 22, is consulted when a
variant or non-variant reading contributes to the textual discussion. In
addition to various works on textual study and the Septuagint text,
grammars such as Gesenius's[5] and studies of syntax such as
Davidson's[6] are used.

The goal of the textual investigation is to arrive at the earliest readings when possible, or when it is impossible (or impossible to judge
whether the reading is early or late), those most probable in light of
their context (as described above). The aim is not an exhaustive
textual study of all possible readings; an attempt is made to establish a

---

1. W. Booth, *The Rhetoric of Fiction* (Chicago: University of Chicago Press,
1961), pp. 71-76.
2. K. Elliger and W. Rudolf (eds.), *Biblia hebraica stuttgartensia* (Stuttgart:
Deutsche Bibelstiftung, 1967–77).
3. R. Kittel (ed.), *Biblia hebraica* (Stuttgart: Wurttembergische Bibelanstalt, 9th
edn, 1954).
4. A. Rahlfs, *Septuaginta*, II (Stuttgart: Wurttembergische Bibelanstalt, 4th edn,
1950).
5. E. Kautzch and A. E. Cowley (eds.), *Gesenius' Hebrew Grammar* (Oxford:
Clarendon Press, 2nd edn, 1910).
6. B. Davidson, *Hebrew Syntax* (Edinburgh: T. & T. Clark, 3rd edn, 1910).

workable text. This study will be mostly exempted from later comparisons due to its specialized aim, for such an undertaking is considered preliminary to the following analyses. The form-critical section will consist of three inquiries. First, an attempt is made to identify the genre of Psalm 18, and this involves a consideration of the liturgical elements of the psalm. Further, Psalm 18's royal themes and vocabulary are examined. Preliminary readings identify Psalm 18 as a thanksgiving hymn, but since it cannot be ascribed to a definite *Gattung* without an in-depth analysis, the second inquiry compares Psalm 18 to others of its assigned *Gattung*. Here, the designation 'form' takes on an added meaning. While it primarily refers to genre, this second inquiry assumes that the word designates the individual structure of a psalm. This is compared with and contrasted to the typical form (genre), an ideal category, to discover the psalm's conformity to this *Gattung*. Within the process, the private or corporate nature of the psalm's discourse is revealed. This final task is related to the third inquiry: the critic has now reached the stage for determining a *Sitz im Leben* for the poem. Factors to be considered are summed up briefly in these three divisions: (1) sociological factors, (2) implied connections with the cult in the mood and intention of the poem, and (3) direct connections with the cult by way of vocabulary. An effort is made to examine the mood and intentions of the poem as well as other internal features for any clues to its cultic use. This examination is part of an attempt to amass enough information to present a clear and intelligent defense for a single liturgical setting.

As Hermann Gunkel provides the form-critical model for the study, so James Muilenburg provides the model for rhetorical criticism. Muilenburg conceives of rhetorical criticism as a discipline complementary to form criticism.[1] With two such closely related approaches, some overlap is inevitable. While constantly seeking to avoid needless repetition, this study makes use of rhetorical criticism to expand the findings of form criticism, though it is not necessary for each investigation to begin with form-critical findings. Rather, assuming the poem's identity with a particular *Gattung*, the unique features of that psalm are examined, and contradictions, confirmations, and expansions of form-critical findings duly noted.

A rhetorical study begins by defining the boundaries of the text.

---

1. Muilenburg, 'Form Criticism'.

One guideline for the endeavor is words or phrases which are repeated. The text may be divided into several smaller units. The 'fit' of these individual units into larger ones gives the text its unique definition, although this conjunctivity is by no means the only defining feature. The most important rhetorical device isolated in this task is *inclusio*. The interpreter must remain alert and creative to identify thematic and structural clues to unity/disunity.

Once the basic length and divisions of the passage are decided, the structure of the psalm is analyzed; the overall pattern of the complete unit is sketched; poetry is searched for lineation, meter, and stanzas; and key words or controlling phrases are identified. Consequently, the rhetorical shape of the psalm is apparent and may be compared with others of its genre in preliminary fashion. Since rhetorical criticism highlights the distinct nature of the literary unit, contrast is often more important than similarity and the uniqueness of the psalm draws the focus. Following this original rough outline, the psalm is repeatedly read with intense concern for detail (the New Critics' 'close reading') as the investigator examines each specific rhetorical feature. Some literary devices are identified as essential to the coherence of the text (e.g., alliteration, parallel structures and chiasmus, metaphors) while others are incidental. When the passage is read aloud, certain aural qualities which are not evident in silent reading are discovered. The isolation of mnemonic devices also provides insight into the oral origins and nature of the psalm. When textual difficulties interfere with the rhetorical study, they are examined, though emendations on rhetorical bases are made with critical reluctance. Having examined the character of the text following these guidelines, the critic is prepared to explicate the text according to its structural outline.

Following the structural study, a discussion of themes is in order. The psalm's perspective on time, space, direction, motion, and the like is explored. The narrative may 'move' through time, or geographically, or spatially in some other way. Key words are also important as they represent clusters of meaning associated around individual images. All major literary devices such as those outlined above are re-examined to show how they are related to the themes. Although the dictum that form and content cannot be separated finally proves true, the interpreter is forced to attempt some separation of formal structure and theme to understand the peculiar nature of their interrelationship. Accordingly, the emphasis within this section of the study is upon the topics covered semantically in the devices rather than the mechanical structure of the devices themselves.

After such a thorough reading, the critic may illustrate the interaction of the motifs within the unit through an original interpretation beginning with a general statement concerning the way themes intertwine. A concise explanation of the transitions is in order, followed by a full outline with commentary and discussion characterizing the combination of structure and theme to produce a unique message. This serves to show the unique artistry involved in the psalm as a specific example of its *Gattung*.

The reader-oriented study of Psalm 18 begins with a series of readings which were suggested by the theorists consulted and shaped by the nature of Psalm 18 itself. The approaches have been surveyed and selected on the basis of their applicability to the Psalms, as well as the demonstrable findings they yielded.

Each of these readings may also be applied under the rubric of rhetorical criticism as outlined above. Indeed, some of these concerns will likely be a part of the rhetorical 'close reading'. However, the results of such readings would be seriously limited if they were gained solely by a rhetorical study. The reason is that the rhetorical analysis focuses upon the text. In this section, the centrality of the reader guides the research with respect to its presuppositions, method, and processing of findings. The difference between the two orientations may be roughly summarized as the difference between structure and effect. Rhetorical studies analyze the structure of the immanent 'text'; reader-response criticism examines the effect the text engenders in the reader. The two methods share a concern for structure: the first, as an end in itself; the second, as one of several factors that shape the response of the reader. Although the concern for structure is shared by the two methods, the implications of that structure lead them in divergent directions.

The readings pursued for the literary analysis include four major searches. The first notes the point of view of the text including each change of voice. The second isolates each individual speech act utterance contained in Psalm 18. The third distinguishes literal from non-literal statements, including the identification of metaphorical statements. The fourth examines the entire psalm for its general rhetorical features. A specific portion of this broad examination subjects selected sections of the psalm to an experimental reading employing

Fish's 'affective stylistics'. In preliminary fashion, within this fourth search, previous readings are analyzed and co-ordinated.

Following the readings, each feature isolated is examined as one member of a network of signals that guides a reader's response to the text. This network is investigated from the standpoint of several structural matrices. First, a sequential pattern is searched out which rests in part on Fish's strategy of affective stylistics.[1] The effect of each word is built on the word before and partially determines the effect of the word to come. This technique may also be applied to larger units to show the progression of the reading process. The second matrix involves an attempt to identify sporadic, dense, attention centers which do more to determine the reader's response than other sections. Whereas the previous matrix emphasizes progression, here the central concern is emphasis displayed in a concentration of written clues which performs in much the same way as a cluster of metaphors built on one central image. However, these signals include many and various structural devices in addition to metaphor. The third matrix is explicated by positioning the clustered devices according to their relative importance, with the aim of identifying one or more core matrices. Such a pattern may be expressible in a single word or phrase, but such dynamic unity cannot be assumed. The critic allows for the possibility of multiple or conflicting centers of directives for the reader by identifying a matrix (or matrices) that is (or are) as multi-faceted as required to provide a basis for the explication of the overall structure of the psalm.

The network of signals within a text, in addition to forming the structural pattern evinced above, also determines the nature of the reading process. Certain signs may accelerate or impede the reading process. Expectations may be fulfilled or frustrated. Similar signs determine the reader's involvement in the text. At times, the reader becomes a full participant in the narrative. At other times, the reader remains distant and must relate to the text externally. This analysis is a most important one for the Psalms because of their varied perspectives and references. At times, the reader will be referred to actions, places, states, and the like which are within the text itself. At other times, references will be made to persons, history, and literature which are external to the text. A careful, unbiased reading isolates

---

1. Fish, *Is There a Text in This Class?*, pp. 21-67.

many features which determine the range and depth of the reading experience.

The network of signals evidenced by a text includes an implied view of the reader.[1] The identity of this ideal reader can be discussed by means of a series of questions concerning the text's perspective. Is the reader alluded to as an individual or as a group? Is the implied reader a historical figure (past, present, or future history), or simply a typical one? Is this person or group specific, or one of several possibilities, or to go even further, is the reader a universal figure? Is the reader a member of an elite group, or a common individual? These examples are far from exhaustive. Other perspectives may be suggested by the distinct nature of the text.

After sketching the patterns that the various readings suggest, a more specific concern is investigated, namely, the nature of speech acts in Psalm 18. First, the basic categories (locutionary, illocutionary, and perlocutionary) will be applied to each utterance. This study gives rise to an identification of the dynamics at work in the speech acts of Hebrew poetry, with emphasis on Psalm 18. The first attempt is made to characterize the special nature of the psalm from this point of view. Fundamentally, the interest centers on distinguishing Psalm 18 as (1) literature rather than ordinary language, (2) poetry rather than prose, and (3) a member of a unique class of utterances in addition to its general character as literature and poetry. These three elements provide the framework for the entire study of speech acts. The focus of inquiry narrows from the general to the particular as the study is pursued.

The next, more narrowly focused, step is to place each speech act within one of Austin's 'families' to examine how each works in context. There are five, designated as 'verdictives, exercitives, commissives, behabitives, and expositives'.[2] Searle's subsequent proposal is roughly parallel and perhaps more easily comprehended. His 'categories of illocutionary acts [are]...assertives, directives, commissives, expressives, and declarations'.[3] Assertives tell how things are done, directives attempt to get others to do things, commissives are used to commit oneself to doing something, expressives are used to air personal feelings, and declarations actually perform changes in the

1. Iser, *The Act of Reading*, pp. 34-38.
2. Austin, *How to Do Things with Words*, p. 151.
3. Searle, *Expression and Meaning*, p. viii.

world. As these categories are pointed out within the psalm, its special nature should become clearer.

Following such a thorough study of the individual utterances that compose the psalm, the nature of the entire speech act situation may be examined. In essence, this study looks at Psalm 18 as an extended speech act. The heart of the investigation lies in the question, when Psalm 18 is considered as a performative utterance, what special characteristics does it show? The paradigm which determines what is 'special' and what is not is in the first case ordinary speech, secondly, literature, and thirdly, poetry. This contemporary approach is supplemented by an investigation of the psalm's ancient Near Eastern context in the following section.

Analysis of Psalm 18 as a speech act assumes there is a person performing the act—the performative actor. This actor is not equivalent to the author; instead the actor corresponds to Booth's implied author.[1] In Psalm 18, different actors present themselves at distinct points in the poem, but a single performative actor will be identified, if possible. If not, Psalm 18 cannot be considered a single speech act unless individual actors can be related in some integrated fashion. The performative actor is viewed in terms of the clues within the text which aid in identification, the aims implied in the performance, and the relationship to the reader, among other things.

The identification of the performative actor(s) may suggest a certain view of the psalm, and the several options available are investigated. From the speech act perspective, Psalm 18 and all other literature may be considered mimetic discourse—the speech act in question mimics an ordinary speech act situation. From this viewpoint the speech act in question becomes a 'pretended performative':[2] 'pretended' not in that the speech acts are unreal, but rather in that the context for the speech acts is more or less a manufactured one.[3] The speech acts function normally, but the speech situation is strictly literary. One possibility is to read Psalm 18 as an imitation of a private prayer with 'David' as the actor. Another approach might suggest a worship situation with multiple actors and thanksgiving as its aim. These and other possibilities deserve discussion, and following a thorough discussion

---

1. Booth, *The Rhetoric of Fiction*, pp. 71-76.
2. Searle, *Expression and Meaning*, pp. 65-70.
3. M.L. Pratt, *Toward a Speech Act Theory of Literary Discourse* (Bloomington: Indiana University Press, 1977), p. 96.

of Psalm 18 as mimetic discourse, a single approach is suggested and defended.

Speech act theorists from the very beginning have underscored the importance of context. No speech act can be properly understood outside of its context. One of the problems in discussing literature as ordinary speech acts is that the context of literature is restricted. In speaking, place, expression, tone of voice, eye contact and other factors determine the nature of the speech act. While the reading contexts of such documents as Psalm 18 vary considerably, the words remain basically the same. The contexts of the statements of Psalm 18 call for special attention.

Only common reading conventions enable critics to talk about texts understandably. Literature can only be read by members of interpretive communities who agree in an implicit way on how reading is done. Such communities can only find within a text what their interpretive systems allow them to find. Again, Fish's point is overstated,[1] but the basis of his argument is undeniable. The community context radically affects the notion of literature, for interpretive strategies are a direct effect of societal identity, especially with respect to the way that society uses its texts.

If the previous sentence goes somewhat beyond Fish's theory, it is with a purpose. Psalm 18 in its early Hebrew context was constructed and read within the milieu of a predominantly oral society. Further, the use made of the text in ritual performance doubtless affected its shape in multiple ways; in certain ways, these contextual concerns belong to a form-critical study. They call for attention from the reader's perspective as well, for these conventions have limited the understanding of the Psalms by tying them to specific acts of worship or speech. The speech acts of Psalm 18 need analysis not only as literary speech acts but also as words spoken in some ancient context. The perlocutionary act performed by the utterance was a ritual enacted with an awareness of its efficacy. With this in mind, an effort is made to identify some of the early 'reading' conventions associated with the Psalms as evidenced in Psalm 18.

Ritual and *reading* are the key words that specify the ancient and contemporary approaches to Psalm 18. Once the ritual context is reconstructed (not in any positivistic sense), this model is compared

---

1. Fish, *Is There a Text in This Class?*, pp. 303-55.

with the contemporary reading. Such terms as 'David', 'servant', and 'salvation' may assume weakly related or even conflicting connotations due to the shift of context. Psalm 18 is currently employed with totally different ends than in its previous contexts. When these are isolated, the result is not only a contemporary reading of Psalm 18 but also a comparative view which locates the reading more accurately in its relative context. This attention to context completes the reader-oriented study.

Finally, comparisons are drawn among the three approaches. Admittedly, any comparison is somewhat unbalanced in that two proven methods are being compared with one preliminary investigation. One weakness of the reader-response approach should be noted in advance: there is no standard, tested methodology, nor does this study attempt to form a single model such as those employed for form and rhetorical criticism. Having said this, another standard for comparison suggests itself: the approaches may be tested in terms of their results. This suits the purpose of this study much better, since the primary interest is in the substantially different offerings of the new method. Three guidelines for comparison are suggested: (1) each approach is analyzed in terms of what it purports to do; (2) each method's limitations are assessed; and (3) the results of each study are weighed in light of what they offer for the study of Psalm 18. The concluding section of the study provides a final evaluation of the reader-response approach to Psalm 18 incorporating a summary of important contributions and limitations. An extended discussion of potential applications of reader criticism and speech act theory in future Psalms study follows.

Chapter 2

TEXTUAL STUDY

The most distinctive textual feature of Psalm 18 is its parallel in 2 Samuel 22. This poem comprises the lengthiest of poetic parallels in the Hebrew Bible; consequently, textual critics have largely been interested in the ways that these two copies differ. Since this study is not primarily interested in the psalm as an object of textual study, such readings will be discussed only as they affect a translator's work.

Introduction

The relationship of the two texts must be considered, however briefly, in order to place each in perspective. Differences between the two are slight. This leads one to confirm Oesterly's appraisal that both stem from the same original, and accordingly, that the differences are in transmission only.[1] Cross assumes that editors at some point began a harmonization of the two passages which was never completed,[2] but this thesis is difficult to confirm; several verses do show the evidence of conflation. He favors 2 Samuel 22 with regard to age, arguing that 2 Samuel 22 contains archaic features (notably a lack of vowel letters) which show a northern Israelite dialect before the fall of Samaria, but that 'in the light of the complex history of the transmission of the Hebrew text, individual cases of archaic spelling do not constitute sufficient evidence for the dating of biblical passages'.[3] So, the proof is inconclusive.

Freedman's statistical method for dating Hebrew poetry may be of some help in determining the dates; את, אשר, and ה are prosaic

1. W.O.E. Oesterly, *The Psalms* (London: SPCK, 1953), p. 162.
2. F.M. Cross, Jr, 'Studies in Ancient Yahwistic Poetry' (PhD dissertation, Johns Hopkins University, 1973), p. 125.
3. Cross, 'Studies', p. 126.

features according to this system. Later copyists tend to incorporate these elements into poetry since they copy poetry as though it were prose.[1] Disregarding the introduction, a count of these articles seems to favor Psalm 18 as the purer copy of the poem. Only the definite article occurs in Psalm 18, where it is written five times. In each instance, it is appended to אל or an adjective modifying אל. Such a use of the article in appellatives is not the conventional way it was applied, but the name האל could have drawn the articles to its adjectives by attraction. At each occurrence, its use could be described as atypical of its standard prosaic employment. In 2 Samuel 22, on the other hand, אל occurs twice, and the article occurs five times, twice in the name האל. Ruling out the use of the article in conjunction with the divine title, the definite article appears three times in 2 Samuel and not at all in Psalms. Also, the sign of the direct object occurs twice in Samuel. The samples are too small to claim irrefutable evidence of Psalm 18's priority, but the count leads toward that conclusion.

Putting aside the comparative dating of the parallels, most contemporary critics would agree with the assessment that 'in its original form [Psalm 18] is one of the most ancient in the Psalter'.[2] The Psalm is described as late pre-exilic in its present form and no reason exists to disbelieve its earliest association with David.

Dahood, one of the most conservative scholars with respect to the dating of the Psalms, uses the Septuagint in his argument for the antiquity of most of the Psalms. He dates Psalm 18 as early as David, arguing that the unfamiliarity of the Septuagint with biblical poetry (especially its metaphors) implied a long gap between the earliest compositions and Septuagintal translations.[3]

The Septuagint plays a secondary role in this textual study in accordance with Dahood's statement above, and following the rather standard procedure of employing the Greek copy of Psalms only in those cases where an original variant is otherwise implied. This involves much selective reading since the copying and recopying of the Psalter for liturgical purposes (Jewish and Christian) multiplies the potential for variant readings. Add to this the consideration that,

---

1.   D.N. Freedman, 'Pottery, Poetry, and Prophecy: An Essay on Biblical Poetry', in J.R. Maier and V.L. Tollers (eds.), *The Bible in its Literary Milieu* (Grand Rapids: Eerdmans, 1979), pp. 79-80.

2.   Oesterly, *Psalms*, p. 162.

3.   M. Dahood, *Psalms 1* (AB; Garden City, NY: Doubleday, 1966), p. xxx.

due to this complex history of transmission, more Greek manuscripts of Psalms are extant than any other book of the Hebrew Bible and the difficulties of using Septuagintal readings as a primary tool for textual criticism of the Psalms become apparent. According to Sidney Jellicoe, Rahlfs recognizes six textual families in Septuagintal Psalters.[1] To avoid complicating the issues unnecessarily, the Septuagint will be used to make emendations only where it provides a clearly preferable reading, and variants will be mentioned only when considered equally plausible.

Several poems within the Masoretic Text itself share the imagery and vocabulary of Psalm 18. The most important for the textual critic is Ps. 144.1-10. It contains references to Yahweh as צורי, מפלטי, מגני and משגבי, as in Psalm 18. Psalm 144 also repeats much of the theophanic language found in 18.7-17 with many identical phrases. The Song of Moses in Deuteronomy 32 also refers to Yahweh as צור. He is depicted as a warrior whose angry fire consumes his enemies. Most of the elements of the 'Yahweh as warrior' theme may be located in the Song of Deborah in Judges 5. A weaker link can be established with Micah 7, where Yahweh delivers the righteous and conquers the enemies of the righteous. The presence of so many related passages helps to confirm the early origins of this poem. In certain cases, these passages (especially Psalm 144) also help by providing alternative readings in cases of corruptions or confused variants.

The textual discussions to follow will make use of the aids mentioned above. *BHS* will be used as the fundamental text, with suggested readings based on its textual notes, informed and expanded by suggestions from various scholars. A verse-by-verse analysis of the text accomplishes the goal of arriving at an original rendering of the entire psalm. In addition to standard text-critical bases, decisions are founded on the following literary assumptions: (1) that the text possesses its own integrity apart from external systems such as lineation, meter and syntax, (2) that sense (semantics) is finally the primary determinant for text-critical decisions, and (3) that the local and general semantic contexts of the document in question are to be taken into account as a major guide for text-critical choices. These literary concerns supplement the textual study in a manner that makes it better suited for the specific aims of this investigation.

---

1. S. Jellicoe, *The Septuagint and Modern Study* (London: Oxford University Press, 1968), p. 297.

Textual Notes and Translation Notes

Discussion on each verse is organized into two sections. The first is designated 'text' and concerns corruptions and variant readings. The second is designated 'translation' and concerns the various possibilities of a given consonantal text. Verses are enumerated according to the Hebrew text and not as in English; consequently, the lengthy title comprises v. 1. English verses following the title will consequently bear a number which is an increase by one.

Text: Verse 1a

The first variant of the psalm occurs with ומיד. 2 Sam. 22.1 and other manuscripts read ומכף which is the parallel term. ומכף would certainly be expected, and this makes the present reading difficult to explain as an error. The principle of *lectio difficilior* favors ומיד. Likely, this led Kraus to suggest a nonparallel translation, offering the meaning 'and in particular'.[1] His reading seems somewhat extreme, especially since 'from the hand of' is such a stock phrase when used of deliverance. It is better to identify ומכף as the secondary reading which arose as a result of its previous occurrence. Craigie describes ומיד as a variant arising from differences in transmission.[2]

Text: Verse 1b

Dahood translates שאול as 'Saul,'[3] which requires a change in pointing only; Sheol is mentiones in v. 6. Problems arise with the unusual 'hand of Sheol', although this does occur in Hos. 13.14 and Ps. 49.16. The strongest argument against Dahood's translation is that there is no tradition supporting it.

Text: Verse 2a

Most critics agree that ארחמך does not belong in the original poem. It is a *hapax* in the *qal* in Hebrew, although it occurs in Assyrian, Aramaic, and Syrian with the meaning 'love'.[4] Briggs recommends

1. H.-J. Kraus, *Psalmen*, I (BKAT, 15; Neukirchen–Vluyn: Des Erziehungsvereins Neukirchen, 1972), p. 138.
2. P.C. Craigie, *Psalms 1-50* (WBC, 19; Waco: Word Books, 1983), p. 168.
3. Dahood, *Psalms*, p. 104.
4. C.A. Briggs and E.G. Briggs, *A Critical and Exegetical Commentary on the Book of Psalms* (ICC, 1; Edinburgh: T. & T. Clark, 1901), p. 151.

dismissing the phrase ארחמך יהוה חזקי as a gloss, since it is also absent
in 2 Samuel 22. Others[1] changed the reading to ארממך, 'I exalt you'
(Pss. 30.2; 145.1; and Isa. 25.1). In spite of its strangeness, ארחמך is
retained in accordance with Buttenwieser but for different reasons.[2]
His recommendation is based on the presence of an Aramaic equivalent. An even stronger objection is based on the principle of
maintaining the integrity of the text. The line 'fits', and there is no
more reason to omit it here than to add it to 2 Samuel 22. The translation 'love' rather than 'have compassion' draws attention to unique
usage (Yahweh is the object, not the subject).

Text: Verse 3a, b
Many scholars[3] advocate the omission of יהוה viewing it as a repetition
from the previous verse. 2 Sam. 22.3 begins with אלהי instead,
omitting אלי from the following phrase. Dahood prefers the rendering
in Ps. 18.28, considering that the divine title יהוה אלי was simply
separated to strengthen the parallel between the two units.[4] The
objection that יהוה is a repetition cannot be maintained. Dittography is
not a possiblity since the word חזקי stands between the two occurrences. The only logical objection to יהוה is a metrical one. This study
soundly rejects emendation offered solely *metri causa*. Such a practice
would delete a good portion of poetic texts simply to bring them into
conformity with rigid systems of balance which are at best uncertain.
The reader will remember that semantics has been identified as the
final determinant.

Objections to משׂגבי are of the same nature. Some scholars[5] wish to
delete it, and *BHK*[6] goes even further by recommending that the final
phrase of 2 Sam. 22.3 be added after the deletion. No textual evidence
is present to support such a reading, and the motivations for both

---

1.   Including H. Gunkel, *Die Psalmen* (Göttingen: Vandenhoeck & Ruprecht,
5th edn, 1968), p. 68; Kraus, *Psalmen*, p. 138; H. Schmidt, *Die Psalmen* (Tübingen:
Mohr [Paul Siebeck], 1934), p. 27; Cross, 'Studies', p. 140; and BDB, p. 933.
    2.   M. Buttenwieser, *The Psalms Chronologically Treated with a New
Translation* (Chicago: University of Chicago Press, 1983), p. 463.
    3.   For example, Gunkel, *Psalmen*, p. 68; Schmidt, *Psalmen,* p. 27; Briggs and
Briggs, *Psalms*, p. 151; and Oesterly, *Psalms*, p. 164.
    4.   Dahood, *Psalms*, pp. 104-105.
    5.   Gunkel, *Psalmen*, p. 68; and Kraus, *Psalmen*, p. 137.
    6.   Also Briggs and Briggs, *Psalms*, p. 152.

emendations are entirely metrical. The addition of material from Samuel would add another half line to form a quatrain.

Translation: Verse 3c

צורי has been identified as a divine appellative, since the Septuagint at times renders it θεός.[1] In this case, the Septuagint reads βοηθός μου ('my assistant') which is not a literal rendering and so adds credence to the suggestion that the word functions as an appellative. One further consideration adds weight to the idea: the word צורי is almost certainly used as a name in Deut. 32.4, 15, 18, 31. The difference in sense is slight, but it is preferable to capitalize 'Rock' as a name.

Text: Verse 4a, b

Some connect מהלל with the previous verse. The Syriac has it modifying, 'my glorious refuge'.[2] Although מְהֻלָּל is *pual* and thus passive, the Septuagint reads αἰνῶν, an active participle with the same meaning. Several textual critics find מְהֻלָּל problematic. Kraus objects to it for syntactical reasons, preferring מְחֹלָל, the *poal* participle used in Isa. 53.5—'pierced'.[3] Schmidt reads מְהֹלֲלִי, which makes it clear that this verb refers to the Psalmist as offering praise.[4] Gunkel's reading is unique, for his translation, '*vor meinen Spöttern* [mockers]' would be written with the same consonants as Schmidt's but with the alternative meaning—'to be boastful' (מְהֹלֲלִי).[5] There is little reason to make the matter so complicated. When מהלל is understood as a reference to יהוה, the translation 'who is worthy of praise' works very well.[6]

The textual notes in *BHK* show אֲשַׁוֵּעַ (שׁוע to cry out for help) as the proposed reading in place of אֶשָּׁעַ. אשׁוע does occur in v. 7 but there is no support for its presence in v. 4.

1.   Briggs and Briggs, *Psalms*, p. 151.
2.   J.J.S. Perowne, *The Book of Psalms* (1 vol. edn; Grand Rapids: Zondervan, 1976), p. 218. Dahood also attached it to v. 3; *Psalms*, p. 105.
3.   Kraus, *Psalmen*, p. 138.
4.   Schmidt, *Psalmen*, p. 27.
5.   Gunkel, *Psalmen*, p. 69.
6.   So rendered by Perowne, *Psalms*, p. 218; and Dahood, *Psalms*, p. 105.

Translation: Verse 4a

Buttenwieser suggests the interesting translation, 'I cry, "Glory to God!"' for מהלל אקרא יהוה. He understands מהלל יהוה as a battle cry.[1] Unfortunately, his suggestion is not confirmed by several other occurrences of the *pual*. Only here and in 2 Samuel 22 could it possibly be construed as a battle cry, and even in these units, the context does not provide sufficient support for the reading.

Text: Verse 5a, b

The majority of critics prefers 2 Samuel's משברי־מות (22.5) to חבלי־מות. Jon. 2.6 may be cited in support of the phrase as recorded in Samuel.[2] Perhaps חבלי was picked up from the following verse in error.[3] In spite of the apparent consensus, two good reasons exist for preserving the present reading. First, חבלי־מות is not a *hapax*. On the contrary, it is described by Kraus as 'a common word pair evinced by חבלי־שאול.'[4] Secondly, the sound of חבלי nearly echoes that of ונחלי in the second half of the line, as noted by Craigie.[5] The change that has been proposed is based almost solely on a desire for a closer correspondence between the two parallel units, חבלי־מות and נחלי־בליעל. Actually, no evidence exists that Hebrew poetry shows a higher degree of parallelism to be an ideal or norm in the formation of texts, and a certain amount of inconsistency is expected. Lacking a variant in the Psalms text to lend weight to the emendation, the reading חבלי־מות may be confirmed. This word pair also occurs in Ps. 116.3.

Another approach to the text is suggested by Douglas Stuart. He recommends that the words מות and בליעל be exchanged one for another.[6] This would yield the stock phrases חבלי־מות and נחלי־מות. The present reading could be explained as an error in taking dictation. The suggestion is quite plausible, but again, textual evidence is lacking.

---

1.   Buttenwieser, *Psalms*, p. 463.
2.   Perowne, *Psalms*, p. 220.
3.   Accordingly, Cross, 'Studies', p. 141; Buttenwieser, *Psalms*, p. 463; G.B. Gray, *The Forms of Hebrew Poetry* (Hoboken, NJ: Ktav, 1972), p. 296; Schmidt, *Psalmen*, p. 27; Gunkel, *Psalmen*, p. 69; Briggs and Briggs, *Psalms*, p. 152; Oesterly, *Psalms*, p. 164; and Dahood, *Psalms*, p. 105.
4.   Kraus, *Psalmen*, p. 138.
5.   Craigie, *Psalms*, p. 169.
6.   D.K. Stuart, *Studies in Early Hebrew Meter* (Missoula, MT: Scholars Press, 1976), p. 183.

Translation: Verse 5b

The meaning of בליעל remains unclear. Its context in vv. 5 and 6 places some helpful parameters on its translation. It may be construed in a physical sense (referring to death or destruction), or in a moral sense (referring to wickedness or lawlessness). The Septuagint reads ἀνομίας (lawlessness) but other renderings fit the context better. In the historical books of the Hebrew Bible, it is often read as a name. Briggs advocates a moral connotation, reading 'ruin, destruction'.[1] Most etymologies favor a derivation from בלי יעל ('without value, worthless'). A literal translation built on this etymology will not fit here. Thomas proposes a new etymology based on בלע (to swallow), and translated it as a noun, 'swallower', referring to Sheol as the pit which engulfs, thus, 'abyss'.[2] Cross goes one step further to translate it as a name, 'Swallower', referring to a Canaanite deity.[3] When the context is considered, the RSV's translation 'perdition' seems the best option; the context also lends support to Thomas's etymology.

Text: Verse 7a, b

The notes in *BHK* suggest that אשוע be deleted and אקרא be substituted. Scholarship does not follow Kittel's suggestion, however, for most understand the second אקרא as a scribal error of repetition.[4] Cross uses the appearance of different verbs in the Septuagint and the Vulgate as evidence.[5] Textual evidence for a change in Psalm 18 is somewhat weak. The reading אושע (I was saved) of the Cairo Geniza is rejected outright, since a passive verb cannot be employed without further changes. The difference in sense is slight, but אשוע is preferred over the use of 2 Samuel 22 as a standard for corrections.

In the second line of v. 7, לפניו overloads the meter and syntax. The easiest option is to omit it.[6] Its presence is explained in various ways, including the claim that לפניו was an explanatory gloss added to

---

1. Briggs and Briggs, *Psalms*, p. 152.

2. D.W. Thomas, 'בליעל' in the Old Testament' in J.N. Birdsall and R.W. Thomson (eds.), *Biblical and Patristic Studies in Memory of Robert Pierce Casey* (New York: Herder, 1963), pp. 18-19.

3. Cross, 'Studies', p. 105.

4. For example, Briggs and Briggs, *Psalms*, p. 152; Gray, *Forms of Hebrew Poetry*, p. 295; and Cross, 'Studies', p. 144.

5. Cross, 'Studies', p. 144.

6. Oesterly, *Psalms*, p. 164; Kraus, *Psalmen*, p. 138; and Schmidt, *Psalmen*, p. 27, among others.

prevent an anthropomorphic reading of באזניו.[1] It is also suggested that
the original combination of two variants (לפניו תבוא תבוא באזנו) was
lost due to haplography.[2] One might expect to find help in the text of
2 Samuel 22, but in Samuel the line is abbreviated and reads באזניו
ושועתי. Weingreen proposes omitting לפניו from Psalms and adding
תבוא to Samuel. He surmises that in Psalms the note, לפניו, was
originally written above the line to show that אזן referred to hearing
rather than literally to ears.[3] Although the evidence, once again, is too
weak to justify deletion, in this case לפניו must be omitted. It cannot be
translated smoothly and when translated simply 'to him' adds nothing
to the meaning of the passage. However, to preserve it in the Hebrew
is important due to the anthropomorphic nuance it focuses upon.

Text: Verse 8a, b, c
The word ותגעש occurs only here in the *qal*. Slight support exists (two
manuscripts) for reading *hithpael*. The Masoretic reading may be preferred as the more difficult.[4] Stuart describes the pointing as unclear
and recommends the *piel* form.[5] The consonants in 2 Sam. 22.8 are
the same, but the pointing is for the *qere*, וַיִּתְגָּעַשׁ. The least troublesome option is to read the text as it stands.

In spite of alternative readings in Samuel, Ps. 18.16, and several
other manuscripts, no good reason is present to discard ומוסדי הרים.
Although other expressions are more frequent, this one is perfectly
acceptable. Other options include (1) accepting Samuel's מוסדות השמים
on the principle of *lectio difficilior*[6]; (2) using v. 16 as a pattern,
giving מוסדות תבל; and (3) following Deut. 32.22 to support the present reading. In Deut. 32.22, הרים also corresponds to ארץ which
occurs in the first part of the verse. A few critics accept the current
Masoretic Text.[7]

The final third of the line, ויתגעשו כי-חרה לו, is usually considered a
gloss. Kraus notes that it disturbs both the sense and the meter of the

1.   Gunkel, *Psalmen*, p. 69; and J. Weingreen, *Introduction to the Critical Study
of the Text of the Hebrew Bible* (London: Oxford University Press, 1982), p. 81.
2.   Cross, 'Studies', p. 144, followed by Stuart, *Studies*, p. 183.
3.   Weingreen, *Introduction*, pp. 82-83.
4.   Briggs and Briggs, *Psalms*, p. 152.
5.   Stuart, *Studies*, p. 183.
6.   Briggs and Briggs, *Psalms*, p. 153.
7.   Including Cross, 'Studies', p. 144, and Craigie, *Psalms*, p. 169.

line, and consequently omits it.[1] Some difficulty arises from the use of the verb חרה when the adjective אף would be expected.[2] The awkwardness is apparent, and nothing is lost by its omission.

Text: Verse 9a

Gunkel omits the last three words, describing גחלים בערו ממנו as variant to the addition described above.[3] In spite of the obvious parallel, these words may be retained as original. They are syntactically correct and fit the context much better than the previous gloss. The addition to v. 8 may have arisen in anticipation of this phrase in v. 9, and that interpretation is followed here.

Translation: Verse 9b

The standard practice of translating the singular אף as plural is observed in the effort to achieve a smoother, more idiomatic style. Further, the ב prefix to אף will be translated 'from' in keeping with the parallel מפיו. Although this is not the most common meaning for ב, it is not rare.

Translation: Verse 10a

Cross suggests the unconventional translation 'He spread apart the heavens...', comparing their opening to that of a giant curtain.[4] This suggestion seems well within the range of meanings assignable to נטה. It also fits the context well, since the idea is passage from one domain to another.

Text: Verse 11a

Several texts, including 2 Sam. 22.11, read וירא for וידא. דאה suits the context.[5] The reading 'he was seen' introduces a passive element that is foreign to theophanies. וירא likely arose from a confusion of ר for ד in copying.[6]

The conjunction of וידא with its near synonym ויעף leads scholars to

1. Kraus, *Psalmen*, p. 138; also Gunkel, *Psalmen*, p. 69.
2. Briggs and Briggs, *Psalms*, p. 153.
3. Gunkel, *Psalmen*, p. 138; followed by Kraus, *Psalmen*, p. 138.
4. Cross, 'Studies', p. 145.
5. Briggs and Briggs, *Psalms*, p. 193.
6. Briggs and Briggs, *Psalms*, p. 193; Cross, 'Studies', p. 145; and Dahood, *Psalms*, p. 107.

consider them combined variants.[1] Cross translates 'he flew' only once.[2] His omission would be better received if there were textual warrant for it. As it stands, the double verbs can be attributed to the 'wordiness' of Hebrew poetry.

Translation: Verse 11b, a
The double occurrence of verbs meaning 'to fly' in the middle of the verse leads to questions on the different nuances intended. The first, עוּף, carries the basic sense 'to fly'. The primary consideration is the more specific connotations that דאה adds. The word is used primarily of birds of prey, often describing their swooping to capture game. The context of the theophany supports this interpretation, as 'the LORD' is descending from the heavens. The translation 'he swooped down' provides the best option.[3]

Text: Verse 12a, b, c, d, e, f
Verse 12 and the verse which follows it are the most problematic passages in this psalm. In his *Introduction to the Psalms*, Christoph Barth identifies both as corrupt.[4] Kraus describes v. 12 as 'overloaded and unclear', recommending the omission of certain words.[5] The assessment of v. 12 need not be so pessimistic. Major changes in the text are supported only by 2 Samuel and metrical considerations.

The *waw* conversive in the Septuagint and elsewhere should be read with ישׁת.[6]

סתרו is often dismissed as a variant since it is lacking in Samuel,[7] but the noun does add sense to the half line. It can be retained for lack of texts to support its omission. Gunkel omits סביבותיו instead,[8] which would provide better balance (with a corresponding deletion in the second half line), but support for this emendation is completely

1. Cross, 'Studies', p. 146; and consequently Stuart, *Studies*, p. 184.
2. Cross, 'Studies', p. 146.
3. Briggs and Briggs, *Psalms*, p. 153.
4. C.F. Barth, *Introduction to the Psalms* (trans. R.A. Wilson; New York: Charles Scribner's Sons, 1966), p. 35.
5. Kraus, *Psalmen*, p. 35.
6. Briggs and Briggs, *Psalms*, p. 154; and Perowne, *Psalms*, p. 219.
7. Briggs and Briggs, *Psalms*, p. 154; and Cross, 'Studies', p. 146.
8. Gunkel, *Psalmen*, p. 69.

lacking. To interpret this verse as originally overloaded by one word seems preferable.

Several scholars object to סכתו in search of a noun that is more consistent with the context. Gunkel reads כְּסָתוֹ (his covering).[1] Briggs claims it is a *hapax* form of סכך (to overshadow, screen).[2] No sound reason exists for rejecting the meaning 'booth'.

BHS cites only one manuscript and Samuel as evidence for the reading of חשרת (a mass of) rather than חשכת. חשכת can be considered a 'less common' form of חשׁך.[3] Samuel's reading is the more difficult. According to Cross, the חשכת of Psalms was induced by the previous חשׁך.[4] Buttenwieser also prefers חשרת and, like Cross, translates it as a reference to rain.[5] The concept of darkness is completely consistent with images of coverings or booths. This is the sort of mysterious, primordial language expected of theophanies. The Masoretic Text again offers the best option.

The final two words, עבי שׁחקים, are especially awkward. Gunkel understands them as variants to חשכת־מים erroneously included in the text.[6] Others[7] connect the word pair with the following verse. The complete phrase would be עבי שׁחקים מנגה. This would satisfy metrical requirements nicely but would create the unlikely reading 'thick clouds out of brightness'. Cross suggests that the מ of מנגה is copied from שׁחקים as dittography, and the word נגה is a corruption of נגדו.[8] Stuart, following Cross, proposes these as the original lines:

> עב שחקם נגד   A thick cloud before [him]
> נגד עבם עבר   Before [him] clouds crossed[9]

Unfortunately, there are no variant readings to aid reconstruction. Even the Septuagint gives a redundant text: σκοτεινὸν ὕδωρ ἐν ἀέρων (darkness of water in the air). This only complicates the matter further by offering an additional peculiar interpretation. עבי שׁחקים is out of place whether connected to v. 12 or v. 13. No

---

1. *Psalmen*, p. 69.
2. Briggs and Briggs, *Psalms*, p. 154.
3. Briggs and Briggs, *Psalms*, p. 154.
4. Cross, 'Studies', p. 146.
5. Buttenwieser, *Psalms*, p. 463.
6. Gunkel, *Psalmen*, p. 69.
7. Briggs and Briggs, *Psalms*, p. 154; and Cross, 'Studies', p. 146.
8. Cross, 'Studies', p. 146.
9. Stuart, *Studies*, p. 12.

preposition is present to connect it with חשכת־מים, so unwarranted changes are necessary in v. 13 when the word pair is attached to this verse. Without the phrase, no insurmountable problems exist with either verse, nor is there any appreciable loss in meaning.

Text: Verse 13a, b, c, d

The text of 2 Samuel 22 omits עביו.[1] This does provide for smoother reading, but no external reason exists to give Samuel's text priority here. Prior and subsequent contexts are consistent with the appearance of clouds. Although this makes עביו suspect, it also proves it consistent. αἱ νεφέλαι appears in the Septuagint. The lack of textual evidence for omission is the deciding factor.

עברו is replaced in 2 Samuel 22 with בערו. Perhaps metathesis has occurred, changing the Psalms text.[2] Briggs defends this position with the claim that the Psalm's misreading drew the reference to clouds to complement the thought of עבר in this context.[3] Once again, the only basis for changing the present text is in its parallel in Samuel. As to the difficulty of עברו, the first two words of the line, מנגה נגדו, actually prevent a smooth rendering. These are present in both Samuel and Psalms and go uncontested by variant readings. They are equally problematic when read with עברו or בערו. To give precedence to 2 Samuel is to rule out an equally plausible option without good grounds. Weingreen speaks for the antiquity of both texts; he points out that both begin and end with the same words, and he surmises that a portion of the complete text had been omitted in Samuel. Weingreen posits עבועברבר as the original text. The copyist might have read עבועבר as a senseless dittography and omitted it. He then simply read בר as defective for בער.[4] The explanation is, of course, too pat. No amount of explanation can provide clarity, so it seems preferable to allow the texts to stand as they are, as far as this is possible. The lack of clarity may then be dealt with through translation rather than emendation.

One further discrepancy exists between v. 13 in 2 Samuel 22 and in Psalm 18; the word ברד does not occur in Samuel. B.S. Roberts attributes the psalm's repetition to dittography from the preceding

1. Kraus, *Psalmen*, p. 139; and *BHS* also favors the omission in Psalms.
2. Craigie, *Psalms*, p. 169; and Briggs and Briggs, *Psalms*, p. 155.
3. Briggs and Briggs, *Psalms*, p. 155.
4. Weingreen, *Introduction*, p. 74.

עברו,[1] and the critic is left without basis for its omission (excepting Samuel). Gunkel points out that the word נחלים appears in four different phrases including Ps. 18.13b, 2 Sam. 22.13, Ps. 18.9c, and Ps. 18.14c. He describes the phrase as 'corrupted, reshaped, and restored'.[2] These recurrences well illustrate the fluidity of Hebrew poetry, and each may be retained as an example of artistic license.

Translation: Verse 13b

A list of various translations of v. 13, or portions of it, will provide a sense of the diversity its interpretation brings about:

1. At the brightness that was before him, his thick clouds passed away—or, separated themselves—(so that) hail and coals of fire issued from them.[3]
2. His clouds went forth, viz., hail and coals of fire.[4]
3. Out of the brightness before him, there passed through his cloud hailstones.[5]
4. From the brightness before him, he leads his clouds.[6]
5. At the brightness before, clouds passed over.[7]
6. ...clouds scudded before him.[8]
7. [The brightness before him] dispelled his clouds.[9]
8. Without brightness [his clouds . . .][10]

Certain matters could be discussed at length, such as (1) the possibility of reading עברו 'he leads', or (2) rendering the same word 'scudded', and (3) 'without' as an alternative translation of מן. Rather than complicating the issue further, the first translation (1.) may be accepted as the most straightforward, since it requires less explanation than the others and accepts the Masoretic Text as it stands. Perowne

1.   B.J. Roberts, *The Old Testament Text and Versions: The Hebrew Text in Transmission and the History of the Ancient Versions* (Cardiff: University of Wales Press, 1951), p. 95.

2.   Gunkel, *Psalmen*, pp. 69-70.

3.   Perowne, *Psalms*, p. 219.

4.   Perowne, *Psalms*, p. 219.

5.   Perowne, *Psalms*, p. 219.

6.   Kraus, *Psalmen*, p. 139.

7.   Oesterly, *Psalms*, p. 164. He made undocumented reference to Gressman from whom Gunkel adopted this translation.

8.   Dahood, *Psalms*, p. 108.

9.   Dahood, *Psalms*, p. 108.

10.   Briggs and Briggs, *Psalms*, p. 154.

prefers this version in spite of its 'harsh ellipsis'.[1] The ellipsis is present in the Hebrew of the psalm as well. The RSV makes a slight alteration in Perowne's translation; the phrase 'hail and coals of fire' is the subject, with 'his clouds' as the object of עברו. With this reading, the vagueness of the verse virtually disappears.

Text: Verse 14a, b, c
The Cairo Geniza and several manuscripts omit the verb וירעם; such an omission in the original is doubtful, and practically no Psalms scholar would delete it. This would damage the parallelism, syntax, and semantics of the verse.

The replacement of the ב of בשמים with מ looks suspiciously like a later revision. To explain the addition of the less conventional ב prefix is more difficult. The Cairo Geniza favors frequent variations, but agrees with the Masoretic Text in this instance. This lends confirmation to the problematic form in the current text.[2]

The closing phrase, ברד וגחלי־אש, is completely out of context; its omission in 2 Samuel 22 and in the Septuagint (Psalm 17) provides further weight to support its deletion. Of the critics consulted for this study, only Craigie would retain it. His reasoning was not based on textual considerations but on rhetorical grounds. Its repetition from v. 13, he claims, creates an effective parallel. Considered from this perspective, the phrase would liken the aural imagery of v. 14 to the visual imagery of v. 13; even Craigie admitted that the phrase may have arisen due to dittography.[3] In the context of v. 14 it seems extraneous.

Text: Verse 15a, b
The Cairo Geniza, Septuagint, and 2 Samuel 22 give חץ a plural ending without the personal pronoun. This combination of witnesses should be followed, especially since little semantic difference exists. Cross gives equal weight to both variants.[4] Oesterly favors the substitution of חצים.[5]

The majority of textual critics are unsatisfied with רב in 15b. The

---

1. Perowne, *Psalms*, p. 219.
2. Cross ('Studies', p. 146), Oesterly (*Psalms*, p. 164), and Dahood (*Psalms*, p. 108) favor the reading ב.
3. Craigie, *Psalms*, p. 164.
4. Cross, 'Studies', p. 147.
5. Oesterly, *Psalms*, p. 164.

parallel passage in Ps. 144.6 gives the imperative of the verb ברק. In
2 Sam. 22.15 ברק is read in conjunction with וישלח as the equivalent
of חצים. Kraus favors the simple omission of רב to coincide with 2
Sam. 22.15.[1] Others[2] would emend both Psalms and Samuel to include
a verb and noun built upon the radicals ברק. They believe that the
second occurrence of ברק is omitted in Samuel and misread as רב in
Psalms. Alternatively, רב may be read as a form of the verb רבב ('to
shoot'),[3] but none of these scholars supports such a reading. Dahood
reads רב as רבי, the *piel* of רבב ('to multiply'),[4] but to follow this
option one must reject the Masoretic pointing, without evidence. The
Septuagint reads ἐπλήθυνεν for רב. *BHS* interprets the Greek as
equivalent to ברק; Schmidt also holds this view, accepting the
Septuagint as the correct reading.[5] If the Septuagint is used to arrive
at a Hebrew original, a more literal translation is in order. πληθύνω
is best translated 'to increase' (the Greek equivalent of רבה or רבב)
and it is more consistent to read the adverb or adjective רב in accordance with the Septuagint. Perowne suggests that רב is an adverb.[6] In
spite of the opinion against it, the text stands as it is, since the strongest
reasons for changes are metrical and haplography is difficult to
illustrate. Too many additional changes are necessary to explain how
ברק became רב. The parallel passages are equally unconvincing, for
they, too, must be emended to make the three readings equivalent to
each other.

Translation: Verse 15c, d
Dahood suggests the strange translation of וישלח as 'he forged' based
on an Ugaritic etymology.[7] The translation does not fit the context
well. Craigie questions the meaning 'to forge' for the Ugaritic *šlḥ*,
preferring a literal translation.[8]
    A minority of critics understand the third masculine plural suffix on

    1. Kraus, *Psalmen*, p. 139.
    2. Oesterly, *Psalms*, p. 164; Briggs and Briggs, *Psalms*, p. 155; and Cross,
'Studies', p. 147.
    3. Gunkel, *Psalmen*, p. 70; Perowne, *Psalms*, p. 219; and Briggs and Briggs,
Psalms, p. 155.
    4. Dahood, *Psalms*, p. 109.
    5. Schmidt, *Psalmen*, p. 27.
    6. Perowne, *Psalms*, p. 219.
    7. Dahood, *Psalms*, p. 109.
    8. Craigie, *Psalms*, p. 169.

the two verbs as a reference to the arrows.[1] Briggs argues that the enemies have not yet been mentioned;[2] however, they are clearly mentioned in the statement in v. 4 which leads into the theophany— ומן־איבי אושע. The context, therefore, does not support their view.

Text: Verse 16a

Although it is possible to read אפיקי מים as in Ps. 18.16, אפקי ים (as in 2 Sam. 22.16) is more likely the original. An original reading, אפיקי ים, has been proposed.[3] The מ of the masculine plural was wrongly attached to the following word according to this view. The explanation is too logical to be ignored, and Psalms scholarship has reached consensus on the reading ים.

Text: Verse 18a

מאיבי עז may be considered as plural instead of singular, based on the evidence of the Septuagint and Syriac as well as the Targums. Cross does so to match the following line.[4] If one accepts the title as a definitive factor, there is good reason for leaving the singular. Enemies are mentioned both in the plural and individually (Saul). The textual evidence for עזים is not strong. The plurals of the Peshitta possibly arose in the Septuagint, in which case there is only one reliable witness. According to the notes of *BHK*, the Targums differentiate even further by offering the verb עזו; this makes the parallel complete. The tendency to improve on the form of parallel lines could be understood as a factor which induced ancient variants as well as contemporary interpretations. Accordingly, several translators have supported the verbal rendering.[5] Cross goes further toward completing the parallel by recommending the insertion of כי in 18a.[6] The occurrence of the singular (and absence of כי) in both Samuel and Psalms is convincing evidence of a singular original. Dahood reads עז as a noun with a singular pronoun preceding it in the construct מאיבי,[7]

1. Briggs and Briggs, *Psalms*, p. 135; and Dahood, *Psalms*, p. 109.
2. Briggs and Briggs, *Psalms*, p. 135.
3. Cross, 'Studies', p. 147; and Dahood, *Psalms*, p. 109.
4. Cross, 'Studies', p. 148.
5. Among them, Gunkel, *Psalmen*, p. 70; and Kraus, *Psalmen*, p. 139.
6. Cross, 'Studies', p. 148.
7. Dahood, *Psalms*, p. 110.

but the Masoretic Text is preferred since its inconsistency is within tolerable limits: hence 'from my strong enemy'.

Text: Verse 20a

2 Sam. 22.20 adds אתי to the first half line. The addition of the sign of the accusative brings a metrical improvement.[1] Cross prefers the text of Psalms but acknowledges that it is too short.[2] The shortness of the half line is easier to accept than a reading founded on a parallel passage. Semantically, ויצא למרחב אתי (Samuel) adds nothing to ויוציאני למרחב (Psalms).

Text: Verse 21a

The noun כבוד is given for כבר in some manuscripts and in one recension of the Septuagint (Lucianic). כבר is most likely a defective form of the same word. It is hard to reconcile the idea of כבוד with the context of v. 21. כבר is preferred not only because of the parallel with the preposition within כצדקי as Craigie suggests,[3] but also because כבר provides a smoother reading. The textual evidence is strong but not conclusive, especially since 2 Samuel 22 and Psalm 18 agree.

Text: Verse 22a

The difficult line ולא־רשעתי מאלהי can be clarified by means of emendation. Dahood suggests the reading רשעתים אלהי.[4] This reading eliminates the problems of the preposition מן, but the reading of רשעתים is equally unclear. Albright proposes פשעתי which is used with מן in 2 Kgs 8.20, 22.[5] Strong objections can be made to such a consonantal change without evidence. For this reason, it is best to follow those translators who simply regard it as a pregnant construction.[6] The difficulty concerns translation rather than textual purity.

1. Gunkel, *Psalmen*, p. 70; Schmidt, *Psalmen*, p. 27; and Briggs and Briggs, *Psalms*, p. 156.
2. Cross, 'Studies', p. 148.
3. Craigie, *Psalms*, p. 170.
4. Dahood, *Psalms*, p. 111.
5. Cross, 'Studies', p. 149.
6. For example, Gunkel, *Psalmen*, p. 70; and Briggs and Briggs, *Psalms*, p. 156.

Text: Verse 24a, b
Briggs questions עמו, substituting לו from 2 Sam. 22.24.[1] תמים עם is
not a *hapax*, however; it occurs also in Deuteronomy 18.13. The
meaning 'toward' referring to the deity is not uncommon either; no
compelling reason exists to prefer לו.

ואשתמר is replaced in Samuel by the cohortative ואשתמרה. The
cohortative is preferred by Briggs on the grounds that it is older.[2]
Gunkel prefers it as metrical improvement.[3] It may also be defended
for semantic reasons: the cohortative nuance of self-encouragement
fits the context. Without textual evidence, these arguments are unconvincing; there is finally little reason to prefer the cohortative.[4]

Text: Verse 25
Several interpreters consider v. 25 a repetition of v. 21.[5] That it is
repetitive is undeniable. The question is: is it simply a late duplication
or is it an integral rhetorical device? Given the predisposition of
Hebrew poetry toward *inclusio*, the latter is quite possible. 2 Sam.
22.25 is not sufficiently different to suggest a variant, and without
textual grounds for omission, the text must remain intact.

Text: Verse 26a, b
Gunkel notes that v. 26a 'appears to have lost a word' (namely איש).[6]
BHS follows his assessment by adding איש in the textual notes.
Although the text cannot be altered without attestation, the equivalent
of איש could be added in translation.

While v. 26a suffers a lack of nouns, v. 26b has a surfeit. גבר
overloads the verse metrically and syntactically. Although sometimes
read as נבור instead of נבר, virtually all texts agree on its presence
(including the Masoretic Text of Samuel, and the Septuagint). In spite
of this, a few critics favor its deletion.[7] It is to be retained, since its
awkwardness does nothing to harm the sense of the line.

1. *Psalms*, p. 157.
2. Briggs and Briggs, *Psalms*, p. 157.
3. Gunkel, *Psalmen*, p. 70.
4. Cross, 'Studies', p. 149.
5. Briggs and Briggs, *Psalms*, p. 157; Buttenwieser, *Psalms*, p. 464; Cross,
'Studies', p. 149; and Stuart, *Studies*, p. 185.
6. Gunkel, *Psalmen*, p. 70.
7. Briggs and Briggs, *Psalms*, p. 157; Cross, 'Studies', p. 149; and Oesterly,
Psalms, p. 164.

Text: Verse 28a

כי־אתה is possibly an example of dittography from the following verse, which would lead one to choose 2 Samuel's reading ואת־עם,[1] but it is also plausible that the two lines originally opened the same way. Again, the lack of evidence leads the critic to support the existent Masoretic Text.

Text: Verse 29a, b

Several critics omit תאיר and read נרי as a direct reference to יהוה. Briggs described תאיר as 'a paraphrase'.[2] Dahood read 29a as two complete parallel lines:

> You shine for me:
> My lamp is Yahweh.[3]

Although the meter is improved by Samuel's omission of תאיר, its presence does not corrupt the line. On the principle mentioned before, that sense rather than meter should be the final determinant, תאיר is confirmed.

Text: Verse 30a

Stuart recommends that the entire verse be omitted for metrical and semantic reasons.[4] The verse is tenuously connected to the statements which precede and follow it, but omission is somewhat drastic. Problems center upon two words, ארץ גדוד; the issues concerning ארץ are based upon translation and will be dealt with later. A variant for גדוד (troop) has been found in Lucian's Septuagint: πεφραγμένος (equivalent to Hebrew גדור, 'wall'). Cross is one among several (including *BHS*) who read גדר, following Lucian, but Cross finally omits the entire verse.[5] גדר makes the lines more completely parallel.[6] Rather than make changes on the basis of one Septuagint recension or on a parallel line, it is better to follow the Masoretic Text as closely as possible. Using this strategy, גדוד is the only choice.

1. Gunkel, *Psalmen*, p. 71; and Oesterly, *Psalms*, p. 164.
2. Briggs and Briggs, *Psalms*, p. 158.
3. Dahood, *Psalms*, p. 113.
4. Stuart, *Studies*, p. 185.
5. Cross, 'Studies', p. 150.
6. See Gunkel, *Psalmen*, p. 71.

Translation: Verse 30b

ארץ (as well as 2 Samuel's ארוץ) may be the *qal* imperfect of either רצץ (to crush) or רוץ (to run). Grammatically, neither is better nor worse than the other. The *qibbuts* in a form of רצץ is explained by Gesenius as an original ו which recurred in the imperfect.[1] Most critics seem to favor רוץ, understanding the parallel אדלג to be the deciding factor, as Gunkel notes.[2] Others identify רצץ as the root.[3] To retain גדוד, this reading must be followed; locating רוץ as the root necessitates the alternative גדר. To maintain the closest correspondence to the Masoretic Text, רצץ must be chosen.

Text: Verse 31

The relationship of this verse to Prov. 30.5 and Deut. 32.4, which are partially parallel, provides the basis for textual changes. The interest in v. 31 revolves around its metrical imbalance, for it has an extra parallel line. Cross believes that a colon has dropped out, and uses Deut. 32.4 as a model, suggesting the addition of a fourth parallel line.[4] The weakness of this proposal may be illustrated by a comparison of the two passages. The vocabulary and syntax is quite different as is shown in the following overview:

הצור תמים פעלו	The rock, his work is perfect,
כי כל־דרכיו משפט	Because all of his ways are just:
אל אמונה ואין עול	A God of truth and not iniquity,
צדיק וישר הוא	Righteous and upright is he (Deut. 32.4).
האל תמים דרכו	The God, his way is perfect.
אמרת־יהוה צרופה	The truth of the LORD is proven.
מגן הוא לכל החסים בו	He is a shield to all those who seek refuge in him (Ps. 18.31).

The similarity is not close enough to serve as grounds for textual changes. However, Prov. 30.5 is nearly identical in part as is shown in the following:

1. Kautzch and Cowley (eds.), *Grammar*, p. 180.
2. Gunkel, *Psalmen*, p. 71.
3. For example, Cross, 'Studies', p. 150; Kautzch and Cowley (eds.), *Grammar*, p. 180; and BDB, p. 954.
4. Cross, 'Studies', p. 151.

כל־אמרת אלוה צרופה   Every saying of God is proven.
מגן הוא לחסים בו   He is a shield to those who seek
                                  refuge in him (Prov. 30.5).

A few important sources recommend the deletion of 31b as an addition.[1] This position shows some inconsistency, since 31c is also a part of the Proverbs passage. To use Prov. 30.5 as evidence for textual changes, it is necessary to delete Ps. 18.31b *and* c as added, or to explain the addition of 31a in some way. This is easily accomplished; v. 31a was added to bond this verse to the previous context. It is not necessary to think of v. 31 as a gloss. Conversely, evidence does not warrant such a proposition. This is another case in which metrical considerations have influenced imprudent textual changes.

Text: Verse 32a
A brief comment is in order concerning אלוה. Psalms scholars who substitute אל do so on metrical grounds.[2] אלוה is a relatively rare, but perfectly acceptable, divine title. Stuart describes אל, אלוה, and אלהים as pre-exilic appellatives which were employed alternately as demanded by meter.[3] Translation is the same, then, whether אל or אלוה, but on the basis of *lectio difficilior* אלוה is preferred.

Text: Verse 33a, b
A few textual critics[4] take the more unusual מעוזי of 2 Sam. 22.33 to be preferable to המאזרני. Their reasons for doing so are not clear. Several versions of Samuel give המאזרני, but מעוזי is not given as a variant in Psalm 18; the same is true of ויתן, which Schmidt prefers as a *lectio difficilior* for Psalms.[5] More textual evidence is needed to support such changes.

    Dahood suggested a change in pointing from וַיִּתֵּן to יִתֵּן. This enables him to read יתן as a title—'the one who gives'. This matches האל, providing a title to begin the second half line as well as the first.[6]

1.   Among them, Gunkel, *Psalmen*, p. 71; and Briggs and Briggs, *Psalms*, p. 158.
2.   Gunkel, *Psalmen*, p. 71; and Oesterly, *Psalms*, p. 164.
3.   Stuart, *Studies*, p. 185.
4.   For instance, Cross, 'Studies', p. 157; and Kraus, *Psalmen*, p. 139.
5.   Schmidt, *Psalmen*, p. 29.
6.   Dahood, *Psalms*, p. 114.

Text: Verse 34a

For the sake of sense and syntax, the י of במתי must be dropped. Plenty
of evidence exists for this, as one would expect. A final explanation
could be somewhat more difficult as the anomalous ending is also
found in 2 Sam. 22.34 and in Hab. 3.19 (a parallel passage). Craigie
explains it as dittography,[1] and only Dahood, who reads it as a third
person singular suffix and cites other examples, favors its retention.[2]
Within this context, no suffix is expected.

Text: Verse 35a, b

Several suggestions are offered for readings to replace ונחתה, and the
issue is difficult. נחֵת, the probable root, is not common enough to
grant certainty to the form given here. The Syriac, Targums,
Symmachus, Hieronymus, and 2 Sam. 22.35 offer וְנִחַת, which is
simply the masculine form of the *piel*. The Septuagint reads instead
καὶ ἔθου, apparently identifying the root as נתן. Oesterly changes it to
וַתֻּנַח (*niphal*).[3] It is difficult to reconcile a masculine form with the
verse unless אל is construed as the subject. In their *Lexicon,* Brown,
Driver and Briggs suggest the *hiphil* with this in mind.[4] The *piel* may
also be causative in meaning. This lends weight to the variant, וְנִחַת. To
choose one of the two options for which there is strong textual
support seems the wisest course. The causative sense (with אל as
subject) is the only difference between the two readings. On the
weight of the textual evidence, the variant, וְנִחַת, is preferred. Some
support for this reading is lent by the Septuagint; although it offers a
different verb, אל is the subject in the Septuagint as well.

To improve the meter, some would exclude the word נחושה. It is
absent only in a Septuagint recension of 2 Samuel, so there is practically no textual evidence to support its omission.

Text: Verse 36a, b, c, d

The second person suffix of ישעך is awkward. Attempts to translate in
a way that account for it leave a rough text. The best course is to
follow the consensus and read the first person suffix instead. The
Original Greek Text (as conjectured by *BHS* editors) is the only

---

1. Craigie, *Psalms*, p. 170.
2. Dahood, *Psalms*, p. 115.
3. Oesterly, *Psalms*, p. 164.
4. BDB, p. 639.

witness given for such a reading. The omission of the suffix in the text of the Syriac and Targums produces an acceptable reading, but these texts do not command as much attention as contextual concerns. Another factor which supports the reading יֶשְׁעִי is the occurrence of the same word in vv. 3 and 47.

The omission of וִימִינְךָ תִסְעָדֵנִי is attractive for metrical reasons,[1] and supported by the absence of the words in 2 Sam. 22.36. Actually, the only sound basis for its omission is the preference for the copy of the poem in Samuel as the older of the two. Some points in favor of the retention of the two words are (1) their agreement with the context, (2) the metrical imbalance which remains when they are deleted (i.e. two words instead of three), and (3) the lack of testimony supporting deletion in manuscripts and versions. The words may be retained as an alternative inclusion made by the poet or community responsible for the Psalms copy.

The word וְעַנְוֹתְךָ is unclear and has elicited at least five possible textual renderings. The first, and least attractive, option is to read it literally: 'and your humility/condescension'. The word is not used of the deity elsewhere. The second possibility is that elaborated by Cross who proposes that the root is עני (time). Few acknowledge his reading which results in the translation 'providence' or 'will'.[2] Very few Psalms scholars follow the third possibility, expressed by Buttenwieser: locate the root עֲנֹה and translate 'let it be thy task'.[3] The fourth and most probable possibility gives the priority to 2 Sam. 22.36 which has וַעֲנֹתְךָ—the *qal* infinitive construct of ענה (to answer). This reading calls to mind the psalmist's cry for help in v. 7, and carries the greatest textual support of the possible alterations, although only Symmachus gives a word that is the equivalent of ענה (ὑπακούειν). The Septuagint and Theodotion offer παιδεία (training) which is supposed to have originated with ענה.[4] The fifth possibility is explained by Stuart: since the Qumran text has עֶזְרָתֶךָ, he suggests that the ר was misread as a ו; this, in turn, brought about the change from ז to נ in the second radical.[5] However, if the Qumran variant were an

1. Kraus, *Psalmen*, p. 139; and Oesterly, *Psalms*, p. 164.
2. Cross, 'Studies', p. 154.
3. Buttenwieser, *Psalms*, p. 465.
4. Gunkel, *Psalmen*, p. 209; Oesterly, *Psalms*, p. 164; and Schmidt, *Psalmen*, p. 29 are among those that follow this view.
5. Stuart, *Studies*, p. 185.

important reading, further attestation would be expected. This possibility is preferred by many (including *BHS)* since it allows the smoothest reading. The evidence points to the fourth possibility, וענתך, but the word remains obscure.

The efforts of several critics to emend תרבני are unsuccessful due to the lack of textual support. The addition of לנצח has considerable support, as it is witnessed to by the Septuagint, but this source alone is unconvincing. The Masoretic Text must be followed since its reading in this case is distinct.

Text: Verse 39

The texts of 2 Samuel 22 and Psalm 18 differ considerably on this verse. No changes are necessary in Psalm 18. The textual notes *(BHS)* list a few changes in 2 Samuel 22, but both Psalm 18 and 2 Samuel 22 provide sensible readings with no convincing evidence for a single harmonized reading. This serves to illustrate the difficulty involved with an approach that assumes a single original version of the poem and identifies one copy as superior based on its date and other factors. The two versions of this verse are viable alternatives. They read as follows:

אמחצם ולא־יכלו קום	I wound them and they are not able to rise.
יפלו תחת רגלי	They fall under my feet (Ps. 18.39).

ואכלם ואמחצם ולא יקומון	And I consume them; I strike them down and they do not rise
ויפלו תחת רגלי	And they fall under my feet (2 Sam. 22.39).

Translation: Verse 41a

The word ערף can be understood in several different ways. The RSV translates 'turn their backs'. The word is a noun, but a verb has been inserted by the editors to make the translation smoother. The idea of a fleeing foe is certainly within the range of possible meanings for ערף. Briggs sees it as a more specific reference. He claims it spoke 'of hand on neck of fleeing foe'.[1] He cites Gen. 49.8 where the image is more explicit, but neglects to mention Josh. 7.8 and 7.12 where, as in Psalm 18, there is no reference to the pursuer's hand. Briggs correctly translates ערף 'neck'. Dahood relates the word to the conqueror's

---

1.   Briggs and Briggs, *Psalms*, p. 160.

practice of putting his foot on the neck of subjected foes.[1] This interpretation fits the context, which refers repeatedly to conquered enemies. A translation which is faithful to the text will not spell out the specific practice intended; however, the reading, 'You gave me the neck of my foes', must be understood according to this action or a similar action.

Text: Verse 42a

The construction על־יהוה is problematic as the antecedent of יָשׁוּעַ. Dahood's suggestion that על be translated 'Most High' is unconvincing.[2] The preferable option is to read אל as in 2 Samuel 22,[3] and translate 'to'.

Text: Verse 43a, b

A few Psalms scholars find it necessary to substitute ארץ for על־פני־רוח,[4] but this is needless since either phrase works equally well in this context. This is another case where it seems wise to follow the Masoretic Text rather than suggest changes with scant evidence (2 Samuel and one manuscript).

The word אריקם is certainly out of place in this line. According to BDB, this would be its only occurrence in the *hiphil*.[5] The strongest argument for correction is semantic: 'I will make them empty' makes no sense. Samuel gives two words: אֲדִקֵּם אֶרְקָעֵם. Perhaps the second word was actually an alternative reading of the first which somehow entered the text.[6] Cross outlines the process by which the variant occurred: אדקם was the original reading. It was erroneously written ארקם due to a confusion of ר for ד; this reading, obviously wrong, was subsequently emended to אַרקעם.[7] This interpretation by Cross can be relied on to verify the variant אדקם (from דקק—'to crush').

---

1.   Dahood, *Psalms*, p. 116; also Craigie, *Psalms*, p. 171.

2.   Dahood, *Psalms*, p. 117.

3.   Oesterly, *Psalms*, p. 164; Cross, 'Studies', p. 155; and Schmidt, *Psalmen*, p. 29.

4.   Cross, 'Studies', p. 155; and Oesterly, *Psalms* p. 164.

5.   BDB, p. 938.

6.   Briggs and Briggs, *Psalms*, p. 161.

7.   Cross, 'Studies', p. 155.

Text: Verse 44a

The phrase עם מריבי is corrected by critics who prefer מרכבות (ten thousands).[1] Such a change in the text lacks support of any kind, and it does not provide a better semantic background. The text as it stands is enigmatic, but such textual changes merely trade one problematic phrase for another. The indefinite connotations of the Masoretic Text are to be retained as original.

Text: Verse 45a, b

Cross prefers to point the first word לִשְׁמֹעַ (i.e. as a verb) as in 2 Samuel 22.[2] The pointing in Psalm 18 is also found in Job 42.5 in a similar phrase. Cross's preference seems to be founded on a pre-determined priority for Samuel's text, but the meaning remains the same. יכחשו should probably be read as a *hiphil* or *niphal*, but a better course would be to follow 2 Samuel's יתכחשו.[3] In the *piel*, כחש means 'to be disappointing, to deceive, to fail or to grow lean'. In the *niphal* or *hithpael*, כחש means 'to come cringing'. The latter is much easier to reconcile with the context, and the Septuagint and the Syriac provide further evidence for the change.

Text: Verse 46a, b

The two verbs יבלו and ויחרגו are both questioned, but the suggested changes bring uncertainty to an otherwise clear text. יבלו (they sank) becomes יכלו (they ceased) in one manuscript, the Syriac, and the Targums. In the Septuagint, יִבְלוּ (they grew old) is indicated, while *BHK* gives יבלו שי (they brought gifts). However, none of the evidence for the changes is compelling. The evidence for a change in the second verb is more convincing, though the meaning is unclear. The Cairo Geniza, several manuscripts, and 2 Samuel 22 show ויחגרו (they girded) in place of ויחרגו (they quaked). There are as many suggestions as there are interpreters, it seems, each with less textual evidence than the variant given here. Since the alternative readings are actually more troublesome than the Masoretic Text, the most straightforward solution is to offer the best possible translation of the Masoretic Text. The translation is as follows: 'The sons of foreigners faint away: they tremble from their strongholds.'

---

1. Gunkel, *Psalmen*, p. 73; and Kraus, *Psalmen*, p. 139.
2. Cross, 'Studies', p. 156.
3. Oesterly, *Psalms*, p. 164; and *BHK* suggested the *niphal*.

Text: Verse 48a

On the strength of 2 Sam. 22.48, many critics change וידבר to ומוריד.[1] וידבר can be read with the uncommon meaning 'to subdue', although Briggs claims that דבר with this meaning is Aramaic rather than Hebrew.[2] This argument cannot invalidate the reading וידבר, in part because the meaning 'subdue' is also indicated by the Septuagint (ὑποτάξας). Due to the lack of further witnesses indicated for ומוריד, the Masoretic Text is again confirmed.[3] Further evidence is found in the occurrence of a similar *hiphil* in Ps. 47.4.

Text: Verse 49a

אף is absent in 2 Samuel 22 and a few manuscripts. Gunkel claims that it disturbs the accents but retains it with the translation 'fierce'.[4] Dahood leaves it untranslated, referring to it as a 'conjunction'.[5] Strictly speaking, this is quite possible, but in this context the concept 'anger' fits better.

Translation

		Meter
1	To the choirmaster, from the servant of Yahweh, from David, who spoke the words of this song to Yahweh on the day Yahweh delivered him from the hand of[a] all his enemies, and from the hand of Saul.[b]	
2	He said:	
	I love you,[a] Yahweh, my strength!	3
3	Yahweh[a] is my rock, and my stronghold, and my deliverer;	
	My God, my Rock; [c]I will trust in him—	
	My shield and the horn of my salvation, my secure height.[b]	3+3+3
4	I call upon Yahweh who is worthy of praise[a]	
	And I am delivered[b] from my enemies.	3+2
5	The cords of death[a] surrounded me;	
	And the floods of perdition[b] fell upon me.	3+3
6	The cords of Sheol surrounded me.	
	The snares of death confronted me.	3+3

1. Included are Gunkel, *Psalmen*, p. 73; Cross, 'Studies', p. 157; Oesterly, *Psalms*, p. 164; and Briggs and Briggs, *Psalms*, p. 162.

2. Briggs and Briggs, *Psalms*, p. 162.

3. Craigie is among the critics who preferred the current reading of the Masoretic Text (*Psalms*, p. 234).

4. Gunkel, *Psalmen*, p. 73.

5. Dahood, *Psalms*, pp. 118-19.

7   In my distress I called[a] upon Yahweh;
      And I cried to my God for help.   3+2
      He heard my voice from his temple;
      And my cry [b] fell upon his ears.   3+3

8   Then the earth shook[a] and trembled;
      And the foundations of the mountains[b] quaked [c].   3+3
9   Smoke went up from his nostrils;[b]
      And fire from his mouth was destroying.[a]
      Coals were ignited by him.   3+3+3
10   Then he spread apart the heavens[a] and descended;
      And a storm cloud was under his feet.   3+3
11   And he rode upon a cherub and flew;[b]
      And he swooped down[a] upon wings of wind.   3+3
12   He made darkness his hiding place[b] around him[c]
      His booth[d] the darkness[e] of waters [f].   4+4
13   Out of the brightness before him
      Hailstones[c] and coals[d] of fire pass through[b] his clouds,[a] 3+3
14   Then Yahweh thundered[a] in the heavens,[b]
      And the Most High gave his voice [c];   3+3
15   And he sent[c] his arrows[a] and scattered them;[d]
      And many[b] flashes of lightning and he confused them;[d]   3+3
16   And the channels of the sea[a] were seen;
      And the foundations of the earth were uncovered—   3+3
      At your rebuke, Yahweh—
      At the blast of the breath of your anger.   2+3

17   He sent from on high. He took me.
      He drew me out of many waters.   3+3
18   He delivered me from my strong enemy;[a]
      And from those who hated me, because they were stronger than I. 3+3
19   They confronted me in the day of my distress;
      And Yahweh served as my staff;   3+3
20   And he brought me out to a broad place [a].
      He rescued me because he delighted in me.   3+3

21   Yahweh rewarded me according to my righteousness:
      According to the cleanness[a] of my hands he requited me. 3+4
22   For I have kept the ways of Yahweh,
      And I have not wickedly withdrawn from my God.[a]   3+3
23   For all his judgments are before me,
      And I have not turned his statutes aside from me.   3+3
24   I have been perfect toward him;[a]
      And I have kept myself[b] from iniquity.   3+2
25   Yahweh returned to me according to my righteousness—
      According to the cleanness of my hands before his eyes. 3+3

26 With the kind [^a] you show yourself kind.
    With the perfect person^b you show yourself perfect.   2+3
27 With the pure you show yourself pure.
    And with the perverse you show yourself perverse.   2+2
28 For you^a save a humble people,
    But you lower the eyes of the haughty.   3+3
29 For you light^a my lamp,^b Yahweh.
    My God lights the darkness.   4+3
30 Because with you I can crush^b a troop;^a
    And with my God I can scale a wall.   3+3

31 The God, his way is perfect.
    The truth of Yahweh is proven.
    He is a shield to all those who seek refuge in him.   3+3+4
32 For who is God^a except Yahweh;
    And who is a rock besides our God?   4+3
33 The God who girds me^a with strength;
    And who makes^b my way safe;   3+3
34 Who sets my feet as hinds' feet;
    And causes me to stand upon high places;^a   3+3
35 Who trains my hands for war;
    And enables^a my hands to draw a bow of bronze;^b 3+3
36 And you give me the shield of my salvation.^a
    Your right hand sustains me^b and your answer^c makes me great [^d].3+4
37 You broaden my step under me;
    And my ankles do not slip.   3+3
38 I pursue my enemies, and I overtake them,
    And do not turn back until they are finished.   3+2
39 I wound them and they are not able to rise.
    They fall under my feet.   3+3
40 And you equip me with strength for battle.
    You cause my attackers to fall beneath me.   3+3
41 And you give me the neck^a of my enemies.
    And I critically wound those who hate me.   3+2
42 They cry out and there is no deliverer…
    To Yahweh,^a but he does not answer.   2+3
43 And I rub them away like dust on the wind.^a
    Like the mud of the streets I crush them.^b   3+3

44 You deliver me from the controversies of the people.^a
    You establish me as the head of the nations.
    A people whom I do not know serve me.   3+3+3
45 Upon hearing^a they obey me.
    The sons of foreigners come cringing^b to me.   3+3
46 The sons of foreigners faint away;^a
    And they tremble^b from their strongholds.   3+2

47	Yahweh lives, and blessed be my Rock,	
	And exalted be the God of my salvation—	3+3
48	The God who gives me vengeance	
	And subdues[a] people under me;	3+3
49	Who delivers me from my angry[a] enemies.	
	You exalt me above those rising against me.	
	You deliver me from a person of violence.	2+2+3
50	For this reason I praise you among the nations, Yahweh,	
	And I sing in your name;	4+2
51	Who makes great the victories of his king;	
	Who acts with kindness toward his anointed—	
	Toward David and his descendants forever.	3+3+3

Conclusion: Poetic Features

Since Psalm 18 will be considered as an example of Hebrew poetry, some comments on its poetic features are in order. The presence or absence of these features does not necessarily mark off poetry as distinct from prose; rather, the mark of Hebrew poetry is that these elements are pronounced. The three features of the Hebrew language which are exaggerated in poetry are meter, parallelism, and strophic structure. They are discussed with three purposes in mind: (1) to point out examples of their employment in Psalm 18, (2) to establish the definition of terms used in this work, and (3) to lay the groundwork for subsequent treatments of these issues.

Meter

Since contemporary scholarship will probably never recover the exact formal components of Hebrew metrical arrangements, the question of meter is beyond final resolution. Meter is reckoned in several different ways; G.B. Gray counts meter in terms of stressed syllables.[1] Geller takes a syllabic approach to meter, which he describes as modified by accentual concerns. In spite of the complexity of his model, Geller finds imbalanced lines in twenty-four per cent of his sample.[2] Also, accentual readings actually serve to complicate the issue in his own

---

1.   Gray, *Forms of Hebrew Poetry*.

2.   S.A. Geller, *Parallelism in Early Biblical Poetry* (Missoula, MT: Scholars Press, 1979), p. 371.

estimation.[1] This does not invalidate Geller's method, but serves to illustrate the immediate problems of counting Hebrew meter. In his introduction to Gray's book, Freedman goes beyond both Gray and Geller by claiming that unstressed syllables also play a role in determining meter.[2] He recommends the joint use of Gray's stress count and his own syllable count to inform each other.[3] Stuart uses a count of all syllables to determine meter. In Psalm 18 he identifies at least eight places with textual difficulties (i.e. where meter is imperfect). He also suggests several emendations which aid his metrical reading.[4]

Without major textual alteration, no single method of reckoning meter provides the order and balance generally evoked in the minds of Western readers when the word 'meter' is used. The matter is not quite so hopeless as it seems. The interpreter may adopt one of two attitudes: either the rigid system which determined ancient meter is lost forever, or there was never such a rigid system in the first place. While combing through numerous metrical theories, the latter option becomes increasingly favorable. The concept of meter must be broadened to include not only stresses and syllables, but also a general notion of balance based on semantics as well as form. Lowth recognized this two centuries ago, noting that the nature of Hebrew metrics (in substance and balance rather than feet and complex rhythmical structure) allows a literal prose translation to capture some of their aesthetic nature. But, he concluded, they cannot be effectively recast into another poetic system.[5] James Kugel expresses similar skepticism toward technical expressions of meter when he writes the following assessment of metrical counting in Job:

> It is fairly accurate to say that Job is written in lines of six or seven stresses each, or that there are usually six major words per line, or six to ten syllables per hemistich. But so is it accurate to say that Job is written in the florid style of biblical rhetoric: highly parallelistic sentences, usually consisting of two clauses, each clause stripped to a minimum of three or four major words. It is this writer's conclusion...that of these two descriptions the latter is a better construction of the evidence.[6]

1. *Parallelism*, p. 374.
2. D.N. Freedman, 'Prolegomena', in Gray, *Forms of Hebrew Poetry*, p. xxxii.
3. *Forms of Hebrew Poetry*, p. xxxv.
4. Stuart, *Studies*.
5. R. Lowth, *Lectures on the Sacred Poetry of the Hebrews* (trans. G. Gregory; Boston: Crocker & Brewster, 1829), pp. 35-36.
6. J.L. Kugel, *The Idea of Biblical Poetry: Parallelism and its History* (New

Based on such authorities, the approach to meter in this book will be fluid. The major words (basically nouns and verbs, but including other parts of speech as necessary) have been counted and a six-word pattern has been detected for each set of parallel lines, designated '3+3' meter. '3+3+3' designates those parallel lines which are made up of three members (as in vv. 3, 8, 44, and 51). Other than isolated four-word or two-word half lines, the only other pattern shown in the psalm is a series of four two-word members in vv. 26 and 27, which are, not unexpectedly, overloaded by one extra word in v. 26. When expressed in the above terms, the issue of meter is considerably less complicated.

Parallelism

The basis for parallelism is less enigmatic than that of meter. The terms and propositions first formulated by Lowth remain fundamental, even though some suggest modifications of his tripartite classification of types. The most frequent objection to Lowth's scheme has been regarding the third category. Gray regards the term 'synthetic' as a 'catch-all' and recommends the term 'incomplete' instead. He argues that the essential characteristic of this third, large, category is that a part of the pattern is missing.[1] It is due to Gray's dissatisfaction with Lowth's synthetic parallelism that Freedman notes the complete lack of parallelism in much Hebrew poetry. As a result, he proposes rhythm or meter as the distinctive feature of Hebrew poetry with parallelism as an outgrowth.[2] Lowth's understanding of parallelism is an extremely broad one, and is consequently vague at times.

The importance of equivalency in Lowth's formulation has brought another objection: how can two different phrases be conceived of as exactly equivalent? Freedman points out that in many cases such lines are complementary rather than equivalent.[3] Kugel devotes much of his book to the proposition that parallel lines are neither exactly equivalent nor exactly opposite. Throughout his work, he maintains that the

Haven: Yale University Press, 1981), p. 300.

1. Gray, *Forms of Hebrew Poetry*, p. 59. Geller objected that Lowth's synthetic classification included lines which displayed no parallelism at all: *Parallelism*, pp. 377-79).

2. Freedman, 'Prolegomena', p. xxvi. Gray's view is similar (*Forms of Hebrew Poetry*, pp. 123-24).

3. Freedman, 'Prolegomena', p. xxvii.

key to parallelism is not similarity but differentiation, so that the second line 'by its very afterwardness...will have an emphatic character'.[1] The study of parallelism, according to this view, should accentuate the semantic differences between first and second parallel lines.

Others have found the key to parallelism in the oral origins of Hebrew poetry. Stanley Gevirtz claims that parallelism found its basis in the use of fixed pairs since these were, in essence, parallel terms.[2] Dahood makes many references in his commentary to Ugaritic word pairs also used by the psalmists.[3] A related system known as formula criticism begins with word pairs, but according to Culley is actually based on meter rather than parallelism.[4] The formula consists of a set pattern or meter which the poet used as a framework.[5] The traits of formulaic composition include such features as 'runs' (phrases which recur in slightly different order), an 'adding' style (line is added to line), and 'inconsistencies and contradictions'.[6] Formula criticism would reduce parallelism to little more than the by-product of a repetitious mode of composition.

Lately, emphasis has turned from the mode of composition to the finished product. Recent studies of Hebrew poetry examine the text in its own right rather than seeking out its origins. This, however, has not led to a reaffirmation of Lowth. On the contrary, according to Adele Berlin, 'Most contemporary scholars have abandoned the models of Lowth and are seeking new models for a reassessment of biblical poetry'.[7] These reassessments are built on linguistic theories, and Geller's approach is a prime example. Following Jakobson,[8] he proposes that semantic parallelism be considered in terms of all aspects of the language—sound, sense, and grammar.[9] He criticizes Lowth, and

1.   Kugel, *Idea of Biblical Poetry*, p. 8.
2.   S. Gevirtz, *Patterns in the Early Poetry of Israel* (Studies in Ancient Oriental Civilization, 32; Chicago: University of Chicago Press, 1983), pp. 10-11.
3.   Dahood, *Psalms*.
4.   R.C. Culley, *Oral Formulaic Language in the Biblical Psalms* (Toronto: University of Toronto Press, 1967), p. 118.
5.   *Oral Formulaic Language*, pp. 10-20.
6.   *Oral Formulaic Language*, p. 14.
7.   A. Berlin, *The Dynamics of Biblical Parallelism* (Bloomington: Indiana University Press, 1985), p. 18.
8.   R. Jakobson, 'Grammatical Parallelism and its Russian Facet', *Language* 42 (1966), pp. 399-429.
9.   Geller, *Parallelism*, p. 1.

others, for confusing three aspects of parallelism. They are 'types of parallelism' (e.g. semantic and grammatical), 'degree of parallelism' (e.g. equivalency or non-parallel), and 'rhetorical relationships'.[1] One senses a pretension to 'straighten out the sordid mess that the study of parallelism has produced'. Geller readily admits that it is not so simple to study all aspects of the language of Hebrew poetry, and lists the uncertainties as follows: (1) the original pronunciation, (2) the system of accents, (3) meter, (4) word roots, and (5) syntax.[2] In spite of difficulties, the comprehensive studies that Geller suggests could add extensively to the knowledge of the types and functions of parallelism.

Alter's approach to parallelism is slightly less ambitious. He accepts Kugel's estimation of parallelism as more than simple reiteration.[3] In so doing, he rejects the narrow, confining view that would stifle his approach to the Bible as literature. Similarly, Alter reject fixed word pairs as the central feature of parallelism, and his argument is convincing: 'The elaboration and variegation of supposedly fixed pairs lead one to suspect that oral composition was at most a fact of the prehistory of our texts'.[4] Alter favors the consideration of Hebrew poetry as a 'potpourri' of several distinctive patterns which alternate in importance from one example to another—meter, syntax, semantics. All are included in the designation 'parallelism'.[5]

Definition of Terms

After the above synopsis, it may seem surprising that in the matter of the definition of terms, Lowth provides the background. Perhaps the primary reason for this is that his proposals comprise the first systematic treatment of parallelism. The difficulty with competing terms is compounded as each theorist adds a new set. A further reason for employing Lowth's terminology is that it is understandable and widely recognized. It will save the trouble of familiarizing the reader with the work of a less notable scholar. Additionally, Lowth's term is broad enough to be 'fleshed out'. They can be informed or reformed by later linguistic research since they are not narrowly technical, and

1. *Parallelism*, pp. 375-76.
2. *Parallelism*, p. 2.
3. R. Alter, *The Art of Biblical Poetry* (New York: Basic Books, 1985), p. 10.
4. *Poetry*, p. 13.
5. *Poetry*, pp. 8-9.

are generally literary in nature. Following Lowth, counterposed phrases will be termed 'parallel lines'. A single phrase (two to four words) is a 'line', which coincides with translation practice, since a single 'line' is generally written as one line in English. The word 'couplet' is used to refer to the next larger unit—a series of two related parallel lines (four lines in English). The terms 'line' and 'parallel lines' are equivalent to the alternative terms 'stich' and 'distich' (sometimes 'couplet'), as well as the terms 'colon' and 'bicola'.

The next larger unit will be referred to as a 'strophe', which designates a series of words larger than a couplet. This use of this term differs from that offered by Charles Kraft, who describes strophic units as either couplets or triads, and designated larger units 'stanzas'.[1] On the contrary, normal usage indicates that the word 'stanza' be reserved for a regularly repeated pattern of lines, a phenomenon which is rare in Hebrew poetry. Kraft described Psalm 18 as a compilation of three or four individual poems united around the theme of praise. He isolated the poems as follows: (1) vv. 8-16 on Yahweh's power, (2) vv. 17-24 on Yahweh as the helper of the troubled righteous, and (3) vv. 32-46 on Yahweh as the God of the warrior (which also contains a secondary poem)[2]. Following the terms used in this study, what Kraft understands as individual poems are to be understood as strophes. The strophic structure of Psalm 18 will be given close attention in the rhetorical study.

1. C.F. Kraft, *The Strophic Structure of Hebrew Poetry* (Chicago: University of Chicago Press, 1938), pp. 105-106.
2. *Strophic Structure*, pp. 105-106.

Chapter 3

FORM-CRITICAL STUDY

Form criticism's perspective on biblical literature is predominantly cultic, recognizing that through its use the poetry of the Psalms is tied to the religious life of the nation Israel. Although nothing in the method itself prevents the application of form criticism to contemporary religious use of the Psalms, the primary concern of form criticism is the cultic origins of Hebrew literature. Much attention is necessarily focused on the distance that separates the 'literary notions' of ancient Israel from the literary theory of the Western world in the nineteenth and twentieth centuries.

Introduction

Gunkel assumes (and there is every reason to believe that this assumption is a sound one) that the idea of literary originality is a modern concept, with the implication that thoughts of an individual author's originality and invention were foreign to the culture and times which produced the Psalms. It may also be helpful to keep in mind that such ideas became standard fairly late in Western culture as well. In any event, those responsible for the Psalms conceived of 'literature' in terms of traditions and conventions. So, to understand Hebrew poetry properly, the modern interpreter must take due account of the context from which it is read. According to Gunkel, this is also true of the contemporary use of the Psalms in worship: 'We must remember that the Psalter is not a book of today, and therefore cannot possibly voice modern thoughts and feelings'.[1]

The recovery of the historical background of the Psalms is not so straightforward a pursuit as it may seem, for form criticism

1. H. Gunkel, *What Remains of the Old Testament and Other Essays* (New York: Macmillan, 1928), p. 114.

originated because historical critical methods were inadequate to explain the Psalms and other literature rooted in oral traditions. The historical origins of the Psalms are all but lost; therefore, criticism must begin with the forms of the literature itself. The study of these forms leads to rational cultic reconstructions.

Slight differences exist between the perspectives of form criticism's two major proponents, Gunkel and Mowinckel. These differences have to do with the relationship of the present-day forms of the Psalms to their ancient use in the cult of Israel. Gunkel sees only a loose connection between psalms in their present form and their cultic origins, for he believes that they now exist in a greatly modified form. Their original cultic roots had been modified by individual use during the exile. Subsequently, they had been reapplied to a later form of the cult. Mowinckel does not feel that such detachment from the cult is indicated;[1] Gunkel's theory is based on an assumption that liturgical forms would be impersonal. Since so many of the psalms intimated an individual dynamic, Gunkel concludes that they had been reworked by individuals prior to their use in the postexilic temple. Mowinckel's opposing view leads him to associate the bulk of the Psalms with actual temple services and festivals. Gunkel, by maintaining greater distance between present and ancient forms, draws the focus upon the forms of the Psalms themselves. Mowinckel, by lessening the distance, draws more attention to the forms of worship.

Background of the Method

The study of forms began rather early in the history of literature (just after Aristotle). The idea of categorizing biblical literature according to type was subsequently applied by such figures as Luther and Eichhorn (1780).[2] Lowth's treatment of the Psalms, which divided Hebrew poetry into the general classes of prophetic poetry, the elegy, the proverb, the ode, the idyllium, and drama, was fairly characteristic of the early classifications.[3] Such an approach has little in common with form criticism as practiced by Gunkel, but it was surely the forerunner of Gunkel's form criticism. Neither Eichhorn nor

---

1. S. Mowinckel, *The Psalms in Israel's Worship*, I (trans. D.R. Ap-Thomas; Oxford: Basil Blackwell, 1962), p. 14.
2. J.G. Eichhorn, *Einleitung in das Alte Testament* (Leipzig: Weidmann, 1803).
3. Lowth, *Lectures*, pp. xx-xxi.

Lowth provided the basis for Gunkel's methodological innovations. The last major spokesman prior to Gunkel was Herder (1782),[1] whose studies were important to Gunkel not only with respect to forms, but also in connection with his entire literary approach. Between the time of Herder's work and Gunkel's intervened the intense preoccupation with historical studies (especially 1830 to the late nineteenth century). Bernhard Duhm's *Die Psalmen* (1899)[2] may be considered the epitome of this historical approach.

Following the appearance of Gunkel's analyses, the discipline of form criticism has grown to encompass several variant applications. The first was proposed by Gunkel's student, Sigmund Mowinckel, who was unsatisfied with the loose connection Gunkel saw between the Psalms in their present forms and their ancient forms. In his own words, 'The psalms are—with very few exceptions—real cult songs, made for cultic use'.[3] In contrast, Gunkel claims that most of the Psalms have been reworked by individuals at some point in time and therefore bear little resemblance to their original cultic form. Mowinckel's thesis prompts him and other interpreters to connect the majority of psalms with a single cultic event; for Mowinckel this event is an enthronement festival.[4] Mowinckel's claims divided form-critical scholarship into two camps: those who refused to identify one theological or ritual center for the majority of the Psalms, and those who employed such a center in their explication of the Psalms.

Gerstenberger points out another deviation from Gunkel's program which was practiced by later critics. Gunkel examines the Psalms for their aesthetic elements (humanistically). Under the influence of von Rad's theology, they were later searched for the word of God within them (i.e. studied theologically).[5] Whereas Gunkel's approach had been cultic, subsequent form critics such as Westermann[6] study the

1. J.G. von Herder, *The Spirit of Hebrew Poetry* (trans. J. Marsh; Naperville, IL: Aleph Press, 1971).

2. B.L. Duhm, *Die Psalmen* (Kurzer Hand-Kommentar zum Alten Testament, 14; Tübingen: K. Marti, 2nd edn, 1922).

3. Mowinckel, *Psalms*, I, p. 30.

4. Weiser reads nearly all the Psalms in connection with a covenant festival (*The Psalms* [OTL; Philadelphia: Westminster Press, 1962]).

5. E. Gerstenberger, 'Psalms', in J.H. Hayes (ed.), *Old Testament Form Criticism* (San Antonio, TX: Trinity University Press, 1974), p. 186.

6. C. Westermann, *Praise and Lament in the Psalms* (trans. K.R. Crim and R.N. Soulen; Atlanta: John Knox Press, 1981).

Psalms according to their theological patterns. This is necessarily reflected in their choices of categories as well as their ascription of individual psalms to certain categories.

Though later form critics differ with Gunkel on the assumptions underlying the approach, they do not differ substantially in their application of the method. The methodology employed in this chapter has already been outlined in Chapter 1. The following comments are offered to fill out that outline. Form criticism as practiced by Gunkel considered the Psalms as a whole rather than individually. They were analyzed in terms of (1) their contexts with respect to the book of Psalms itself, (2) similar material in the Hebrew Bible outside the book of Psalms, and (3) Babylonian, Assyrian, and Egyptian psalms. Form criticism begins, not with an external chronological scheme, but with the Psalms themselves. According to Mowinckel, 'A proper classification must try to find the different fundamental types or species of psalms according to their own rules'.[1] Further, 'Each "literary" type has its special place in life, from which it has sprung'.[2]

In this study, the process has been separated into five stages. They are as follows: (1) identification of the basic thematic units of the text; (2) evincing the relationship of these parts to each other; (3) suggesting a *Gattung* based on the construction of the psalm; (4) proposal of a specific *Sitz im Leben*; (5) description of the particular effect of the given psalm within this setting.

Textual Units

The units of the text are easily identified. Although at times verses which serve as transitions are difficult to place, their precise assignment (or lack of it) will probably not affect the outcome of form-critical work. Division into units, like the previous textual study (Chapter 2), is considered preliminary to the form-critical study itself. These small divisions are not *Gattungen*, but in the interest of thoroughness they are included as the logical units which guide the interpreter in determining genre.

1. Mowinckel, *Psalms*, I, p. 24.
2. *Psalms*, I, p. 26.

Table 1
Thematic Units in Psalm 18

Theme	Verses
Heading	1
Confession of love	2
Summary statement	3
Circumstances of deliverance	4-7
Theophany	8-16
Circumstances of deliverance	17-20a
Assertion of righteousness	20b-25
Yahweh's response to righteousness	26-28
Yahweh's strengthening (for war)	29-43
World reign	44-46
General praise	47-51

Mythic language, most explicitly employed in the theophany, begins in vv. 5 and 6. Such images of death, Sheol, and water are also held in close association in the *Epic of Gilgamesh*. The descent to Sheol is described in this way:

> Difficult is the passage, hard is the way thereto,
> And deep are the waters of death which bar the approach thereto
> (*Gilgamesh* 10.24-25).[1]

Similar mythic themes surface in the Babylonian poem recounting the victory of Marduk over Tiamat (the goddess of the chaos of waters). In v. 5, the floods threaten the chaos of death, but Yahweh is counterpoised, as the one who harnesses the destructive waters.

Psalm 18 shows even clearer relationships to non-biblical Near Eastern literature. Although Lowth[2] and Weiser[3] relate it to the Sinai theophany, it is likely that the loose connections between this scene and Sinai are due to common theophanic expressions rather than direct borrowing. Similarly, Babylonian and Ugaritic deities are described in terms of fantastic natural phenomena. The earth trembles at the sound of Baal's voice.[4] The same was said of the Babylonian god

---

1. E.P. Dhorme, *Choix de textes religieux assyro-babyloniens* (Paris: Lecoffre, 1907), pp. 284-85, cited by Driver, 'Psalms', p. 145.
2. Lowth, *Lectures*, pp. 77-79.
3. Weiser, *Psalms*, pp. 189-91.
4. J.B. Pritchard (ed.), *The Ancient Near East: Anthology of Texts and Pictures*, I (Princeton: Princeton University Press, 1958), p. 106.

Ramman when he was angry (*Gilgamesh*, 4.35-38).[1] Just as Yahweh is
pictured descending on a cloud in v. 10, Baal is frequently referred to
as 'Rider of Clouds' in Ugaritic texts.[2] In an Akkadian creation epic,
Marduk mounted a 'storm-chariot' to ride against Tiamat,[3] and used a
'flood-storm' to defeat her.[4] Yahweh's 'arrows' also correspond to
similar images in connection with Marduk.[5]

Although the assertion of righteousness is a recurring theme in
biblical poetry (see Pss. 17.15 and 41.12), the statement in Psalm 18 is
a rarer, lengthy confession. A similar, extended assertion of righteousness is found in Psalm 26.

Also of special note are vv. 26 and 27 which lend weight to the
assertion of righteousness by commenting on the nature of the deity in
connection with those who obey him. A noticeable difference exists
between the meter of these verses (basically 2+2) and that of the rest
of the psalm. The two verses form a quatrain, as follows:

עם חסיד תתחסד	With the kind you show yourself kind.
עם־גבר תמים תתמם	With the perfect man you show yourself perfect.
עם־נבר תתברר	With the pure you show yourself pure.
ועם־עקש תתפתל	With the perverse you show yourself perverse (Ps. 18.26-27).

The manner in which it stands out of its context suggests that a four-
line *mashal* has been quoted in support of the assertion.

Structure of the Text

Gunkel sees the lengthiest portion of the psalm (vv. 32ff. by his
reckoning) as a second account of the same circumstances recorded in
vv. 5-20.[6] Setting aside questions of exact division of units, this
approach enables a consistent and continuous reading of both halves of
Psalm 18. When explained in this way, there are no obstacles pre-
venting the consideration of Psalm 18 as a single psalm. With these
comments, the first stage has passed into the second. What is described
in this and the following paragraphs is the relationship of the units.

1. S. Langdon, *The Babylonian Epic of Creation* (Oxford: Clarendon Press,
1923), p. 131.
2. Pritchard, *ANE*, I, pp. 96, 100, 104, 108, 118.
3. Pritchard, *ANE*, I, p. 33 (*Akkadian Creation Epic* 4.50).
4. Pritchard, *ANE*, I, p. 32 (*Akkadian Creation Epic* 4.49).
5. Pritchard, *ANE*, I, p. 32 (*Akkadian Creation Epic* 4.36).
6. Gunkel, *Psalmen*, p. 65.

Since the heading is not included as a part of the song itself, it will be excluded from the form-critical study. Following the heading, vv. 2-4 comprise a hymnic introduction to the psalm with v. 3 as a vague summary of the need and deliverance to be described. Verses 5-7 elaborate on the storyline with special reference to the depth of difficulty (without divine help the actor would have perished). When the psalmist called to Yahweh from his hopeless situation, Yahweh heard, and the stage is opened for Yahweh's response.

The worshipper's plight has already been described with the use of mythological language, and Yahweh's appearance to save is set in a panoply of mythological images. Gunkel comments, at length, on the importance of the theophany, maintaining that the theophany represents a full account of Yahweh's response. This full account of deliverance is central to all thanksgiving songs.[1] Mowinckel sets the theophany in context by describing it as a battle response with the narrative unfolding in the following steps: (1) righteousness is given as the reason for his help; (2) a non-mythical description is then given to show the political nature of the actual problem (vv. 32-42); finally, (3) complete domination of the king over his enemies is shown in the 'peoples whom I do not know' passage.[2]

Since Psalm 18 is divided into two major sections, interpreters seek clues that demonstrate the unity of the psalm. Gunkel locates two distinct closings: the first in vv. 47-49 and the second in vv. 50-51. He concludes that vv. 47-49 (a hymnic introduction in form) corresponds to the hymnic elements of vv. 32-46, while vv. 50-51 (an introduction to a thanksgiving psalm in form) conforms to the pattern of the previous portion of the psalm.[3] In contrast to Gunkel's findings, Weiser finds the keys to the psalm's unity in the individual verses 44 and 49. Each of these verses combines the two emphases of the poem, and, consequently, proves that it is not two poems, but one.[4] Because of the dual nature of the psalm, a final judgment on its unity must be reserved for the discussion of its *Sitz im Leben*.

---

1. Gunkel, *Psalmen*, p. 62
2. Mowinckel, *Psalms*, I, pp. 71-72.
3. Gunkel, *Psalmen*, p. 66.
4. Weiser, *Psalms*, p. 186.

Gattung

There is basic agreement on the *Gattung* of Psalm 18. All interpreters
describe it as a royal song of thanksgiving which conforms to the
structure of an individual psalm of thanks. A few scholars oppose its
classification as a psalm of an individual. Kenneth Kuntz argues that
its identification as a royal song precludes an individual reading;[1]
when judged from this perspective, a royal psalm always expresses
communal rather than individual ideas. The fact that Psalm 18 follows
the form of the individual song of thanksgiving in almost every
respect must not be forgotten; accordingly, it is best describes as a
song of individual thanks offered by the king. Kraus describes Psalm
18 in those terms, but he goes on to distinguish the first section as an
individual thanksgiving and the second section as a royal thanksgiving[2]—a plausible alternative view since it is consistent with the
form of the psalm itself.

Thanksgiving Song
Psalm 18 may be further described as a 'song of victory', although it
does not fit the pattern of the *Gattung* which is so named. Perhaps a
thank-offering was actually offered by the king in conjunction with
the psalm's use.[3] This thesis would be difficult to test; and in opposi-
tion to this view, this *royal* psalm exhibits distinct differences from
those psalms known to have been used in thank-offering ceremonies.
According to Westermann's declarative/descriptive distinction, Psalm
18 is a declarative praise psalm.[4] The deciding factor is whether or
not the psalm was offered in celebration of a specific occasion of
divine help. Descriptive praise includes general praise of Yahweh describing his overall nature. As a declarative psalm of praise, Psalm 18
is an individual song of thanks offered upon the occasion of a military
victory. Gunkel sketches the events recounted in the psalm as follows:

---

1. J.K. Kuntz, 'Psalm 18: A Rhetorical-Critical Analysis', *JSOT* 26 (1983),
p. 4.
2. Kraus, *Psalmen*, p. 140.
3. H.H. Guthrie, *Israel's Sacred Songs: A Study of Dominant Themes* (New
York: Seabury Press, 1966), p. 12.
4. Westermann, *Praise*, p. 83.

In this manner he [Yahweh] answered his prayer during war and defended him against his enemies (Ps. 18.18-20); he equiped him for his combat (cf. Ps. 144.1) and granted him victory, even world dominion (Ps. 18.33ff.); therefore he shouts his song of thanks (Psalm 18).[1]

A thanksgiving psalm opens with praise of Yahweh (vv. 2-3), and continues with a description of the trouble (vv. 4-7). This description of trouble includes a call to Yahweh and records Yahweh's hearing of the cry; the thanksgiving psalm then depicts Yahweh as savior (vv. 17-21). Normally his salvation is proclaimed for the edification of others (perhaps in vv. 28, 31), and at times the thanksgiving psalm closes with the mention of a thank-offering.[2] Psalm 18 clearly contains much material which is extraneous to the psalm of thanksgiving. In particular, the theophany, the assertion of righteousness, and the preparation for battle are lacking in Mowinckel's generic scheme, though the inclusion of these elements does not dictate against the assigned *Gattung*. Rather, the discrepancies point out the depth of the variations which can be used to shape a form. The essence of a psalm of thanksgiving can be reduced even further than in the above outline. The entire psalm may be considered an expansion of a single, pithy sentence,[3] notably, the one which occurs in v. 3.

Verses 25-28 and 30-31, at first glance, show no relationship to the summary sentence. These assertions of righteousness point out that Yahweh has acted in accordance with his usual behavior; that is, it is his practice to deliver in these circumstances.[4] Although such statements do not normally occur in thanksgiving songs, they are relatively frequent within the broader category of the psalms of praise.

There are several elements common to different types of praise psalms which mark Psalm 18 as distinct among thanksgiving psalms. The most notable inconsistency concerns the two major halves of the psalm (vv. 1-31 and vv. 32-51). In Westermann's words, 'the

---

1. H. Gunkel, *Einleitung in die Psalmen* (Göttingen: Vandenhoeck & Ruprecht, 1933), p. 156.

2. This model is presented in Mowinckel, *The Psalms in Israel's Worship*, II (trans. D.R. Ap-Thomas; Oxford: Basil Blackwell, 1962), pp. 32-39.

3. Westermann, *Praise*, p. 108; and K. Koch, *The Growth of the Biblical Tradition: The Form-Critical Method* (New York: Charles Scribner's Sons, 1969), p. 162.

4. Westermann, *Praise*, p. 111.

declaration...is changed into description',[1] or, as accounted by the categories of Gunkel, the first half of the psalm follows the type of the song of thanks, the second section is hymnic. The presence of general praise in a specific song of thanks is one mark of the uniqueness of Psalm 18. The two juxtaposed *Gattungen* heighten the sense of praise by broadening it from specific thanks for deliverance to general acclaim for Yahweh's overall nature.

Royal Song

Psalm 18 has been identified as a royal song of thanksgiving. The preceding discourse focused on the nature of Psalm 18 as a song of thanks, but the *royal* aspects of the poem need to be addressed. Many of the peculiarities of Psalm 18 may be explained in terms of its royal character. Essential to this discussion will be the origination of royal psalms, their use in the cult of Israel, and their dual individual–corporate nature.

Royal psalms had their origination in kingship ideology common to much of the ancient Near East, and Gunkel describes the royal songs as characterized by 'extravagance'.[2] He finds merit for this explanation in the understanding that they were borrowed from dominant nations and applied to a relatively insignificant one. He lists the exaggerated elements as follows:

(1)   The claims of the king, concerning the length and scope of reign;
(2)   The claims for Yahweh, regarding his power;
(3)   The king's closeness to Yahweh; and
(4)   The king's faith and fairness.[3]

When the royal psalms are considered from such a perspective, they assume the character of ritually expressed hopes and dreams. They are not intimations of the actual status of the king and nation, but are records of Israel's international aspirations. Although an extreme expression of this view invites debate, the basic assumption cannot be denied: claims for king and kingdom are exaggerated in the royal psalms. Verse 44—'You establish me as the head of the nations'—may be cited as a typical example.

1.   *Praise*, p. 117.
2.   Gunkel, *What Remains of the Old Testament*, p. 90.
3.   *What Remains of the Old Testament*, p. 90.

Such claims were attributed to the monarch of Israel. The royal psalms are considered the oldest psalms due to their association with kingship in Israel, evoking the claim that, 'While...some may have undergone modification in the course of transmission, in their original form all are to be regarded as pre-exilic.'[1] In Israel, then, as in other nations, royal psalms were used in conjunction with state festivals which were religious in nature. One such occasion was the celebration of victory in battle. The king and his army returned from war to offer thanksgiving to Yahweh for help in battle. The songs of thanks arising from victories were typically cast as first-person addresses from the king to the deity. The question arises (and it is a question familiar to form critics): to what degree are these songs individual in nature and to what degree are they communal? They were presumably spoken, person to person, between king and Yahweh, but they were spoken within the context of a public assembly, for all to hear.

The answers given to the questions above reveal the broad spectrum of opinions on the personal/public nature of the royal psalms. At one extreme, some interpreters reject the designation 'royal' as a *Gattung* to itself. According to this view, Psalm 18 may be described as a 'royal psalm', but its form-critical type is 'thanksgiving song of the individual'. A related viewpoint is that 'Royal . . . thanksgivings should be placed in between individual and communal prayers of that type.'[2] According to this reckoning, royal psalms of thanksgiving such as Psalm 18 are individual psalms of thanks which were adapted for court use, and should not constitute a separate type.[3] The difference between this view and Gunkel's is quite subtle. Gunkel merely hypothesizes that when the king offered a complaint or a song of thanks, he followed the outline offered by the private songs.[4] On the occasion of military victory, his prayer conformed to the individual song of thanks. For Gunkel, then, it is not so much the content or arrangement that constituted a royal song, but its application to a royal situation.

Due to the special place afforded to kingship in ancient Israel, Mowinckel considers royal thanksgiving songs as public thanksgiving

---

1. T.H. Robinson, *The Poetry of the Old Testament* (London: Duckworth, 1947), p. 129.
2. Gerstenberger, 'Psalms', p. 205.
3. Gerstenberger, 'Psalms', p. 205.
4. Gunkel, *Einleitung*, p. 147.

songs. His disagreement with Gunkel is apparent in the following statement:

> According to its substance, the psalm [Psalm 18] belongs to the public, national thanksgiving psalms. Its form is not due to any imitation of 'private' thanksgiving psalms for the use of an individual, but to a pure cultivation of the king-style as a further development of the earlier national and political thanksgiving psalm with its mixture of collective and individual forms.[1]

Mowinckel's view of kingship necessitates the identification of all royal psalms as corporate psalms, and one must remember that he reads not only the royal psalms, but also many others, in connection with an enthronement festival.

The private/communal nature of royal psalms is often described in terms of the 'I' contained in their lines. Gunkel tends to read the 'I' literally so that a psalm presenting a predominantly first-person perspective is an individual psalm. Mowinckel, as might be expected, reads the 'I' as a royal reference perceived as a communal reference by the ancient reader. Scholarship remains divided on the issue; in any event, even Gunkel notes that royal songs exercise a strong influence on poems of individuals. He suggests that this leads to the consideration of a wider and more influential range of royal psalms; his example is Ps. 18.30, 33ff, which he says 'employed a complete literature of victory songs'.[2] This literature is based in the ancient semitic roots of the Hebrews prior to the present text of the Psalter.

Related Genres

Direct contact with other Near Eastern religions are evident as Psalm 18 is compared to other related genres; for example, the song of victory was associated with a cultic service of thanksgiving, common throughout the ancient world. According to Robinson, songs of victory are not present in their pristine form in the Psalter, because the cultic service disappeared before the exilic compilations of the Psalms.[3] While Psalm 18 echoes the victory songs (especially vv. 33ff), it is not considered as such a song, because the battle description is not detailed and specific. Comparison with a true victory song (Judges 5)

1. Mowinckel, *Psalms*, II, p. 29.
2. Gunkel, *Einleitung*, p. 149.
3. Robinson, *Poetry of the Old Testament*, p. 141.

shows just how similar Psalm 18 is in outline. The Song of Deborah opens with a call to praise (Judg. 5.2, cf. Ps. 18.2-4), and Yahweh's activity begins with a theophany (Judg. 5.4-5, cf. Ps. 18.8-16). The poem continues with a review of the trouble (Judg. 5.6-8, cf. Ps. 18.5-6, 18-19), after which the call to praise is reiterated (Judg. 5.9-11). The record of deliverance completes the song (Judg. 5.12-30, cf. Ps. 18.33-46), and the poem concludes with a curse for Yahweh's enemies and a blessing for his friends (Judg. 5.31, cf. Ps. 18.21-28).

Due to the close connections of Psalm 18 with victory songs, Mowinckel remarks that the psalmist likely studied Egyptian hymn writing.[1] The following is a summary of the narrative of an Egyptian victory song. Pharaoh Rameses II is surrounded by the Hittite army. He appeals to Amon for help on the basis of his devoted service and Amon makes Rameses like Baal in his prowess in battle. Pharaoh overcomes hundreds of thousands of opponents with divine power, though his own army gives him no help on the first day. On the second day, his men join him as bursts of fire from the snake on his head-dress kill the enemy. At the surrender, he is worshipped by the Hittite prince, and his reign of all the world is acknowledged, while the Hittite prince petitions for peace. Upon his return to Egypt, Rameses is greeted with 'jubilees', and his reign over all nations is proclaimed.[2] The song of victory may have served as a model for the later cultic form of thanksgiving psalms, such as Psalm 18, while the older victory songs were 'secular' and originated on the scene of the battle.[3] If the Egyptian psalm is considered the archetype of a song of thanks such as Psalm 18, then the Hebrew poets have removed many embellishments and stylized the original form.

The relationship of the theophany to the entire psalm is dealt with simplistically when Psalm 18 is considered as a development of a victory song: the theophany is an integral part of some of the earliest victory songs. Another perspective on the theophany is presented when it is considered as external to the song of thanksgiving and described as 'inserted'; consequently, vv. 32-48 (the description of Yahweh's granting of military might) are considered an addition of a

1. Mowinckel, *Psalms*, II, p. 72.
2. A. Erman, *The Ancient Egyptians: A Sourcebook of Their Writings* (trans. A.M. Blackman; New York: Harper & Row, 1966), pp. 260-70. In Mowinckel (*Psalms*, II, p. 186) a similar Assyrian song of thanksgiving is cited.
3. Mowinckel, *Psalms*, II, pp. 26-27.

modified song of victory to an original thanksgiving psalm of an individual.[1] These observations may have good grounds, but they are not very helpful; the task is to consider the form of Psalm 18 as it stands. Accordingly, the parts must be related rather than separated. Against the assertion that the theophany occurs as an intrusive element, we can note that theophanies form integral parts of Psalm 18, Judges 5, and Habakkuk 3, and in form, these texts are a thanksgiving song, a victory song and a hymn, respectively. These theophanies have in common: the coming of Yahweh to deliver, the quaking of earth and mountains, water imagery, and associations with battle. The theophany seems to have been used in any context in which the deity's power to save was central, as was true with Israel's neighboring nations. The common mythic elements may be considered even more expansive as shown in the table below.

Table 2
Similarities between Psalm 18 and the
Stories of Baal, Mot and Yam

Psalm 18	*Baal, Mot and Yam*
'Psalmist caught in the cords of Belial' (vv. 5-6).	Mot and Yam reign.
Delivered in theophany (vv. 7-15).	Baal, god of storm, delivers.
Lord conquers waters and earth to deliver (vv. 16-20).	Baal conquers Yam and Mot to end chaos.[2]

Such theophanic elements are central to the thanksgiving song even in its present form.

Similar themes occur in the related genre, thank-offering songs; for example, the passage through Sheol. Thank-offering songs were recited in conjunction with an offering of thanks for recovery from illness or deliverance from other threatening situations. The history of their formulation must be closely related to general thanksgiving songs; Mowinckel believes that general thanksgiving songs were developed from individual thank-offering songs and used in a public context.[3] Psalm 18, for example, would have been developed for royal use on the pattern of a private thank-offering song.

1. Mowinckel, *Psalms*, II, pp. 26-27.
2. Craigie, *Psalms*, p. 173.
3. Mowinckel, *Psalms*, II, p. 27.

Thanksgiving songs and laments are frequently mixed, with one following the other. A trace of such mixture survives in Psalm 18, which shares a single important element with psalms of lament—the statement of innocence. The statement of innocence is uniquely employed in Psalm 18: the claims of innocence in laments typically portray the sufferer as one who was wrongly accused or one who was suffering without just cause for Yahweh's punishment. See, for example, Job 31, Ps. 26.1, Ps. 73.13, and Ps. 142.7 (in Ps. 18, vv. 20-28). Careful reading will demonstrate that they also functioned as arguments which explained that the sufferer was indeed worthy of Yahweh's help. A related ancient genre, the song of innocence, was a distinct type of dirge.[1] Note that in Ps. 18.20-28 the speaker is not pleading for justice, but acclaiming Yahweh's faithfulness to those who are innocent. The statement of innocence works as a didactic statement on the lines of 'this is what Yahweh has done for me and he will do the same for you' (providing you are righteous). From the mouth of David or the davidic king, these words would have carried the force of a royal example encouraging faithfulness to religious traditions and fostering trust in divine help.

The statements of innocence also perform a hymnic function: they extol Yahweh's goodness. Psalm 18 displays several hymnic features. Several additional general features are shared between the character of Psalm 18 as a song of thanks and the character of hymns. Songs of thanks and hymns follow a similar outline which exhibits at least three common elements: (1) a call to praise, (2) a mention of the deeds of Yahweh which deserve praise, and (3) a portrayal of his power in natural forces and past deeds. Songs of thanks offer praise for specific actions of the deity whereas hymns offer praise for God's general nature and activity.

Certain Assyrian prayers open with a hymnic introduction like that of Ps. 18.2-4,[2] but a hymn that uses second-person references to Yahweh is unusual. On the contrary, the hymn is spoken to the world at large.[3] While Psalm 18 may be described as a song of thanks possessing a hymnic character, it cannot properly be considered a hymn of praise due to its personal nature.

1. Gunkel, *What Remains of the Old Testament*, p. 106.
2. C.G. Cumming, *The Assyrian and Hebrew Hymns of Praise* (New York: Columbia University Press, 1934), pp. 53-71.
3. Koch, *Growth of the Biblical Tradition*, p. 163.

The hymnic language of Psalm 18 may be compared to examples from other ancient Near Eastern hymns. In a hymn to Amun-Re, the theme of Ps. 18.6 is repeated:

> You, Amun-Re, Lord of Thebes, are the one who rescues the one who is already in the underworld.[1]

The divine-warrior imagery of the theophany (vv. 7-16) is used of the Assyrian, Marduk, in this section of a hymn:

> The direction of conflict and battle is in the hands of Marduk,
>   the leader of the gods;
> At whose wrath the heaven quakes;
> At whose wrath the deep is troubled;
> At the point of whose weapon the gods turn back;
> Whose furious attack no one ventures to oppose;
> The mighty lord, to whom there is no rival in the assembly of
>   the gods;
> In the bright firmament of heaven, his course is powerful;
> In Ekur, the temple of holiness, exalted are his decrees.
> In the storm wind his weapons blaze forth;
> With his flame steep mountains are destroyed.
> He overwhelms the expanse of the billowy ocean.
> Son of Esara is his name, warrior of the gods his title.
> From the depths is he lord of the gods and men.
> Before his terrible bow the heavens tremble,
> Who the lofty house of death's shadow overthrows and destroys.[2]

In another poem to Marduk, he is compared to other gods:

> What god in heaven can be compared to thee,
> Thou art high over all of them
> Among the gods superior is thy counsel.[3]

Marduk is also pictured as the deliverer of the righteous:

> He has established the god-fearers, to the oppressed he has
>   brought deliverance;
> He has granted favors to the obedient, brought salvation to the
>   just.[4]

---

1. W. Beyerlin (ed.), *Near Eastern Religious Texts Relating to the Old Testament* (OTL; Philadelphia: Westminster Press, 1978), p. 33.
2. Cumming, *Assyrian Hymns*, p. 89.
3. *Assyrian Hymns*, p. 103.
4. *Assyrian Hymns*, p. 140.

The parallels are simply too striking to be attributed to coincidence. Although it is beyond the scope of this study, the possibility of direct connections between the cultus of Israel and that of Assyria should be investigated. With specific reference to Psalm 18, its hymnic language was largely held in common between Assyria and Israel with possible relationships to other ancient literatures. Again, this does not imply that Israel 'borrowed' hymnic language from Assyria. It merely implies close cultural connections between the two countries.

Sitz im Leben

The discussion now turns to the fourth stage of the form-critical process—the proposal of a specific *Sitz im Leben*. Psalm 18 was certainly used in conjunction with some cultic service, and may have been written by temple personnel;[1] more likely, they adapted and expanded an existing song of thanks. Having assumed strong ties with some service of worship, the specific use of the psalm also depends on the identity of the 'I' of the psalm. Weiser identifies the composer as David, or a royal poet during David's reign.[2] In subsequent readings of the psalm, based on this proposal, one would expect a descendant of David to assume the role of the singer.[3] In a later time, after the monarchy, Psalm 18 was likely read historically, as a tribute to the special relationship between David and Yahweh. Surely, the original place of its performance was the Jerusalem temple,[4] as its strong ties with the monarchy indicate. The scenario may be depicted in the following way. After a military victory or according to the time set by a ritual calendar, the king and his entourage would enter the temple in a public worship service. At some point in the worship, the king, or temple personnel on the king's behalf, sang a personal song of thanksgiving which was witnessed by all those attending. The 'I' of the psalm would thus be understood as the direct address of an individual that was offered in a public ceremony and understood corporately, referring to the king who, in turn, represented the populace.

In the course of the worship service, a royal thank-offering may have been given, though references to such an offering were omitted

---

1. Mowinckel, *Psalms*, II, p. 142.
2. Weiser, *Psalms*, p. 186.
3. Gunkel, *Psalmen*, pp. 66-67.
4. Koch, *Growth of the Biblical Tradition*, p. 164.

by later worshippers.[1] Psalm 18 should not be construed as a simple thank-offering song due to its battle imagery and royal overtones. On the other hand, a thank-offering song may have provided the rough outline from which Psalm 18 was composed. Robinson believes that all songs and hymns of thanks arose from the cultic context of the thank-offering.[2] However, there seem to be no traces of this worship practice in the extant Psalm 18.

In setting the scenario above, two cultic contexts were intimated. To decide on a final *Sitz im Leben* the choice must be made as conclusively as possible: was Psalm 18 sung on occasions of victory or on a certain festival day? The answer cannot be as conclusive as desired.[3] In spite of the sound logic which associates vv. 20-24 with the festival, the reader is faced with a pronounced lack of evidence. In several places where national themes are consistent with the line of thought or even expected based upon context, they are absent. For example, the theophany makes no direct reference to Sinai; and the battle language of vv. 32ff. refers to no national campaign. In short, there is no salvation history in Psalm 18, for the victories are personal, the thanksgiving is personal, and Israel is not mentioned.

More credence can be given to the suggestion of an enthronement festival. Aubrey Johnson outlines a festival of worship in conjunction with Psalm 18. It began with a procession to the temple. As part of the temple service, Yahweh aided the Anointed as Rider of the Clouds. He conquered the sea, and took his place in the thunderstorm.[4] The remaining portion of Psalm 18 can also be related to enthronement: Yahweh protected his Anointed in battle. Good reasons are present to reject the identification of Psalm 18 as an enthronement psalm, and various aspects of the psalm are left unexplained by this interpretation. Two concerns are paramount. First, why is an enthronement psalm cast in the form of a thanksgiving song? The expected form would be a salvation-history hymn relating Yahweh's past fidelity to nation and king. Thanks is offered where praise would be expected. Second, why is an enthronement psalm designed so personally? The

1.   Gunkel, *What Remains of the Old Testament*, p. 86.
2.   Robinson, *Poetry of the Old Testament*, p. 135.
3.   Weiser, *Psalms*, pp. 192-93. Weiser attempted to connect at least a portion of Psalm 18 to a covenant festival.
4.   A.R. Johnson, *Sacral Kingship in Ancient Israel* (Cardiff: University of Wales Press, 1955), pp. 64ff., 108.

dialogue displays an individual in relation to Yahweh almost exclusively, and in fact no mention is made of the king's rule. A national psalm would likely contain a congregational response, affirming loyalty to Yahweh and his sovereign. At this point, an objection to the two questions above is anticipated. Some would say that the psalm acquired its present form due to the basic form after which it was modelled; the point is well taken. This royal psalm contains all the elements of an individual song of thanksgiving, but the stated objection to the identification of Psalm 18 as an enthronement festival psalm is more basic. The question simply is: 'why was a thanksgiving song used as the model?' The clearest answer to the question is that the song was to be employed in a service of thanksgiving, and not in an enthronement ceremony.

Since no festival commemorating Israel's victories in battle is known, the previous discussion leads to the conclusion that Psalm 18 functioned as a thanksgiving song on the occasion of military victories. Gunkel describes it as a 'thanksgiving prayer' offered by the king.[1] Eissfeldt offers a more complete characterization:

> [Psalm 18 is] a song of thanksgiving in the form of two parallel movements (vv. 2-13 and 32-51) which the king recites when he returns victorious from the battlefield.[2]

In the case of Psalm 18, the original setting was in a royal service of thanksgiving. After the monarchy, it may have functioned as a similar song of thanksgiving which idealized David (note the heading) and in this way emphasized the national roots of exilic Judaism.

Function

In the fifth, and final, stage of the form-critical process, thematic units of Psalm 18 are to be re-examined in light of the *Gattung* and *Sitz im Leben* proposed. The orientation of v. 1 has, in effect, been rejected. Form-critically the psalm may not be considered as a private prayer, although the poem in its earliest origins may indeed have assumed the form of a private prayer. Its royal theme, especially its ascription to

1. H. Gunkel, *The Psalms: A Form-Critical Introduction* (trans. T.M. Horner; Philadelphia: Fortress Press, 1967), p. 24.
2. O. Eissfeldt, *The Old Testament: An Introduction* (trans. P.R. Ackroyd; New York: Harper & Row, 1965), p. 104.

David, indicates the importance of this psalm to the cult of Israel. Since the individual nature of its language and personal references to the king preclude the possibility of its continued use by various individuals, the individual reader of the poem had to assume a royal identity or at least a national interpretation.

The confession of love is less determinate, for it functions as a hymnic introduction with the unusual 'I love you' substituted for 'I praise you'. Even though the sentence could be uttered by any worshipper, from the mouth of a monarch (or his spokesperson), it perhaps adds a personal touch which is juxtaposed to the summary statement (v. 3). When the two are viewed together, the summary statement (and the entire psalm by implication) serves to explicate the reasons for the love.

The preliminaries function as a call to worship. Verses 5-7 contain the first description of the circumstances which evoked the reactions given in vv. 2-3. The desperation and cry for help brought the congregation into sympathy with the speaker. They identified with him, having assumed his first-person perspective from the beginning. It will be remembered that each worshipper was aware that this empathy was experienced in the king–subject relationship, and consequently, the experience was singularly sacred as well as self-elevating.

The theophany (vv. 8-16) serves to preserve the high standing of the monarch by linking him with an all-powerful deity. Several scholars understand the theophany as an indirect reference to the events at Sinai.[1] Within Psalm 18, a reference to Sinai might be expected, but one wonders why it should be so obscure. There are no straightforward allusions to Sinai, and many elements foreign to the Sinai theophany are included. In Psalm 18, the theophany acts as a testimony to Yahweh's power rather than a historical citation.

From the beginning of the poem to the end of the second account of the deliverance (vv. 17-20a), the nature of Yahweh is highlighted. David (or his descendants) is the secondary focus of the poem. The nature of the king is discussed in vv. 20b-25 with such descriptions as 'cleanness', 'perfect', and 'righteousness' applied to the monarch. The abrupt switch from the king's righteousness to Yahweh's general

---

1. For example, Weiser, *Psalms*, p. 189; and Westermann, *Praise*, p. 101. Weiser supposed that the Sinai theophany was recreated in the cultic festival. Westermann maintained the contrary, stating that the 'differences are more pronounced that the similarities'.

disposition toward righteous persons begins the transition which is made complete in v. 28:

> For you save a humble people [nation].
> But you lower the eyes of the haughty.

The accent on the king's personal moral nature makes it possible for the worshipper to become integrally involved in the ceremony. In contrast to this, the king's moral rule or his enforcement of the laws of righteousness gains more frequent notice elsewhere.

Beginning with v. 26, reference to Yahweh is made in the second person, and this trend continues to the end of the song. In vv. 32-37 attention has turned from the trials and deliverance of the king to the enabling power of Yahweh.[1] Accordingly, the worshipper likely considered the second half of the poem as an extended conclusion to an individual song of thanks. While the description of the circumstances seems to refer to a specific event, vv. 33ff refer to several indefinite actions. Even though the original crisis was perhaps hypothetical, a great difference develops in the second section where no specific time of need is mentioned. From this perspective, the enemies identified in the last half of Psalm 18 appear to be national enemies (cf. vv. 44-46).[2]

Verses 48-49, where the psalm reverts to first-person thanksgiving like that of the first section, summarize the king's public reading.[3] Mowinckel takes the closing of the song literally and ascribes the performance of Psalm 18 to the descendants of David.[4] This is done, in effect, any time a psalm is identified as 'royal', since any king of Israel would be considered a descendant of David.

Conclusion

Psalm 18 strengthened nationalism by associating the king with Yahweh, for allegiance to the nation was allegiance to Yahweh. The king is presented in Psalm 18 as an individual who symbolized the nation as a whole. Yahweh's aid to the king was direct aid to the people, and this perception is the justification for the personal nature

1. Weiser, *Psalms*, p. 195. Weiser commented that in vv. 32-37 'God' is in the nominative to emphasize that the success of the king is due only to him.

2. Johnson, *Sacral Kingship*, p. 108.

3. Weiser, *Psalms*, pp. 48-49.

4. Mowinckel, *Psalms*, I, p. 48.

of the public song. Beyond this, all participants in worship understood the Psalm's function as an *offering* of thanks. Though at one time a thank-offering may have been offered in conjunction with the psalm, in its present form Psalm 18 *is* the offering of thanks;[1] the combined themes of the power of God and the faith of the worshipper blend to bring a forceful picture of everyday reality in God's care. So, the function of Psalm 18 may be denoted as follows: Psalm 18 is a public, royal prayer perceived by all worshippers as an offering of thanks.

---

1. Gunkel, *Einleitung*, p. 273. Gunkel proposed that such an attitude developed relatively late in the history of the Psalms due to the rejection of animal offerings.

Chapter 4

RHETORICAL STUDY

James Muilenburg offered the first concise description of rhetorical criticism in 1968. Muilenburg coined the phrase as a description of the works of well-recognized scholars ranging from Robert Lowth to David Freedman.[1] The figures and techniques upon which rhetorical criticism is based have been noted and at times cogently discussed by virtually all biblical scholars. But the program was substantially new. According to one concise definition, rhetorical criticism is 'the isolation of a discrete literary unit, the analysis of its structure and balance, and the attention to key words and motifs'.[2]

Introduction

One distinct advantage that rhetorical criticism has over most other literary approaches to biblical literature is that it was developed and refined to interpret texts written in biblical Hebrew. As a result, the structure which it finds in the Old Testament is explained according to biblical patterns and read in terms of its biblical context.

Rhetorical criticism analyzes biblical literature in terms of its artistic design. Although in Chapter 1 it was identified as a text-centered approach, as Muilenburg conceives it the author's intention played a prominent role:

> A responsible and proper articulation of the words in their linguistic patterns and in their precise formulations will reveal to us the texture and fabric of the writer's thought, not only what it is that he thinks, but as he thinks it.[3]

1. Muilenburg, 'Form Criticism', pp. 1-18.
2 B.W. Anderson, 'The New Frontier of Rhetorical Criticism', in J.J. Jackson and M. Kessler (eds.), *Rhetorical Criticism: Essays in Honor of James Muilenburg* (Pittsburgh Theological Monograph Series, 1; Pittsburgh: Pickwick Press, 1974), p. xi.
3. Muilenburg, 'Form Criticism', p. 7.

Most rhetorical critics maintain strong ties between author and text; however, there is nothing within the approach itself which in any way binds it to the writer. Rhetorical criticism may be applied to any text as it stands without reference to its author, and in this respect it is text-centered. The text lies before the critic as the object of study, whereas historical origins or contemporary theology are external to the text-centered process which is the basis of the rhetorical approach. Since the method expresses little interest in the earlier forms of the text and its history, it has been characterized as synchronic. Previous textual strategies are, on the other hand, diachronic, since they highlight the text's development as a historical process.

Rhetorical criticism approaches the text as an artistic creation, and evidences an obvious link with aesthetic and stylistic modes of criticism. The turn from historical modes of criticism is equally obvious. If rhetorical criticism does not presuppose history, neither does it dismiss history. Rhetorical criticism cannot be described as anti-historical, but remains ahistorical. With the advent of rhetorical criticism, biblical studies entered a new domain within which the seemingly unlimited possibilities for application are still being explored. The future of rhetorical criticism will be determined by the willingness of biblical critics to branch out into the world of literary criticism within which rhetorical criticism finds its closest parallels. 'Rhetorical criticism...is an art... It should utilize fully the critical and stylistic resources which are employed by the literary world at large.'[1]

Background of the Method

The development of the rhetorical-critical approach was a more subtle phenomenon than may be suggested in the foregoing discussion. The limits of form criticism led to rhetorical studies in much the same way that the limits of historical criticism led to form-critical studies. Muilenburg indicates two major weaknesses of form criticism: first, form criticism focuses upon the patterns of literature to the exclusion of the unique; secondly, form criticism plays down the author and circumstances of writing of a piece of literature, even when sound theories could be offered.[2] Rhetorical criticism answers the first by

---

1. D. Greenwood, 'Rhetorical Criticism and Formgeschichte: Some Methodological Considerations', *JBL* 89 (1970), p. 422.

2. Muilenburg, 'Form Criticism', pp. 5-6.

offering a unique interpretation of one specific example from a *Gattung*, and it answers the second by offering a detailed psychological or formal exposition of the text from which further conclusions may be drawn.

A minority of Hebrew Bible specialists have offered a negative appraisal of the prospects for rhetorical criticism, claiming, for example, 'There is no real "beyond" to form critical psalm exegesis', and implying that the relationship between form criticism and rhetorical criticism is the relationship between an established yet far from exhausted standard and a quickly arisen and already exhausted 'maverick' discipline.[1] Few critics would give form criticism such predominance over rhetorical criticism. On the contrary, others claim that form criticism and rhetorical criticism share similar foundations. For example, both ask identical questions in relation to the text: (1) 'What are the boundaries of the unit?' and (2) 'What is the structure of the unit?'[2] The two disciplines ask the questions for different reasons: rhetorical criticism asks the questions for the purposes of intrinsic analysis; form criticism asks them in order to assign a *Gattung*.[3] Similarly, some have noted that the difference between form criticism and rhetorical criticism may be witnessed in the double meaning of the word 'form'. Form criticism is restricted to investigations that deal with genre (typical patterns); rhetorical criticism comes into play with the unique (individual structure).[4] So, they are separate yet related disciplines, a feature that has led to proposals for the use of form and rhetorical criticism as complementary disciplines applied to a text conjointly.[5] This application is quite plausible but rather unusual. Although the nature of textual interpretation leads to an inevitable blending of methodologies, most interpreters prefer to follow a single dominant approach, supplemented by others, rather than the concurrent application of two divergent styles of criticism.

In addition to its strong relationship to form criticism, rhetorical criticism is also closely related to the discipline named 'stylistics'. This

1. Gerstenberger, 'Psalms', p. 221.

2. P.G. Mosca, 'Psalm 26: Poetic Structure and the Form-Critical Task', *CBQ* 47 (1985), p. 214.

3. Mosca, 'Psalm 26'.

4. R.J. Clifford, *Rhetorical Criticism in the Exegesis of Hebrew Poetry* (SBLSP, 19; Missoula, MT: Scholars Press, 1980), p. 19.

5. For example, Mosca, 'Psalm 26', p. 213.

term is considered less suitable than 'rhetorical criticism' by Muilenburg due to its wider application and ambiguity.[1] In spite of this, 'stylistics' is the term preferred by European scholarship to describe what United States scholars call rhetorical criticism. Stylistics is indeed a much broader designation. Four types of style criticism have been distinguished: (1) style as the search for literary devices, (2) the study of an author's individual style, (3) the study of the style of an entire book or section, and (4) the study of the style of a period (e.g. pre- or postexilic).[2] Hence, 'style' may be used to describe several quite different approaches. Viewing rhetorical criticism as stylistics consequently opens the approach to the area of general literary criticism. Wellek's description of stylistics does not differ substantially from the rhetorical-critical program: 'All devices for securing emphasis or explicitness can be classed under stylistics: metaphors... all rhetorical figures; syntactical patterns.'[3] However, stylistics includes linguistic and aesthetic techniques which are not explicit in Wellek's definition. His definition serves to limit stylistics to those principles which are intended when stylistics is equated with rhetorical criticism.

Specific Application of the Method

Having sketched the origins and parameters of rhetorical criticism, it remains to show its application in this study. Freedman's understanding of the critic's 'attitude' toward the text may be accepted as standard:

> It is difficult if not impossible to draw the line between the conscious intention of the poet and what the attentive reader finds in a poem. On the whole, I think we have given insufficient credit to the poet for the subtleties and intricacies in his artistic creation, and it is better to err on that side for a while. If we find some clever device or elaborate internal structure, why not assume that the poet's ingenuity, rather than our own, is responsible? It is a different matter if it is our ingenuity in restoring or reconstructing the text. In many cases, however, I believe that the process by which the poet achieves an effect is different from the process by which the scholar recognizes and describes it. What is the result of

1.   Muilenburg, 'Form Criticism', p. 8.
2.   Koch, *Growth of the Biblical Tradition*, pp. 15-16.
3.   R. Wellek and A. Warren, *Theory of Literature* (New York: Harcourt Brace Jovanovich, 3rd edn, 1977), p. 178.

conscious effort on our part may be spontaneous in the poet, or second nature. For one who is steeped in the tradition and draws on long experience in creating poems, it is not necessary to start from scratch, and the associations and intricate arrangements, which we discover only after painstaking investigation, may be byproducts of which he is not fully aware, while he centers attention on other aspects of composition. Since there is no way finally to resolve such questions about the intention of the poet, it is a safer and better procedure to restrict or extend ourselves to the visible data and describe what we see there, rather than try to probe the recesses of the poet's mind.[1]

Thoughts of the intention or psychology of the author are considered irrelevant. In this study, the text will be considered an object with its own identity. All patterns and images within the text will be considered artful devices, although this study will stop short of associating the devices with an artist or artists. The line between explicit artistry and the reader's invention will be drawn at that point where the reader's perceptions cease to be demonstrable. In other words, if the critic cannot convince others that a given pattern exists in the sample, then for all practical purposes it does not exist.

Perhaps the most important guideline for discovering artistic design in Hebrew poetry is sound. Rhetorical criticism analyzes Hebrew poetry in terms of its aural qualities, and this is always of primary importance when dealing with oral poetry. The critic must remember that the printed form of the poem arose only as a by-product of its oral transmission. The specific effects engendered by the written forms of the poem (lineation, strophe, etc.) are important only in so far as they reflect audible patterns. The positive side of this issue is that repetition and balance are more easily investigated in written forms. Rhetorical critics have a better chance of discovering the intricate patterns of a poem than audiences which only heard it. Whether informed by the document or by its oral performance, the devices employed are to be searched for their vocal effect. This can only be done in the original language of the poem since a translation would alter the effects. Translation will only be used when imagery, themes, and motifs are discussed, that is, at a level once removed from words and sounds.

In the discussion of the structure of Psalm 18, the aim of this study is not to catalog each and every literary device or formal pattern. The

---

1.   Freedman, 'Pottery, Poetry, and Prophecy', p. 8.

textual features noted in this chapter were discovered in the process of such a comprehensive search. Much selection and editing have been done in order to present a unified scheme with the intention of isolating those features that play the most important roles in the overall structure of the psalm. As the major elements are identified, they will also be interrelated, for any valid rhetorical study evidences the same unity and coherence it finds in the text. Rhetorical criticism is at its worst if it merely identifies and defines an endless list of literary devices employed within a poem. By contrast, the purpose here is to propose a single unified rhetorical reading of Psalm 18. Since the results are synthesized, the method by which the text was originally examined will not always be apparent. The basic approach was simple and straightforward, involving these three steps: (1) the psalm was divided into strophes; (2) each smaller and larger segment within each strophe was analyzed; and (3) each segment (from word to strophe) was examined for its relationship to the entire psalm.

The synthesis of the information gained in the analyses above falls into four categories. First, the boundaries of the text are determined. These boundaries are fairly evident in a book like the Psalter. In addition to locating the limits of the poem during this first stage, a preliminary discussion of the relationships between the opening and the closing, and the body of the psalm, is offered. The second stage examines the formal structure of the text: keywords, alliteration, and strophic organization, as well as many other literary devices, are explicated to illustrate the interrelationship of the parts of the poem on a formal level. In the third stage, the investigation advances from the level of form to that of theme. This stage employs the information gained on the previous level to show the thematic function of the devices; the imagery employed in the poem combines with the formal elements to provide a pattern of progression. The fourth stage completes the analysis with an integrated interpretation. At this time, the several thematic elements of the poem are described in terms of their interrelationships. Final judgments are made regarding the relative importance of textual features investigated, and the unique features and major devices discovered during the explication are used to provide a model for the aesthetic design of the poem. The aim of interpretation is to demonstrate the movement and unity of the psalm in terms of its own structure.

Boundaries of the Text

The first rhetorical-critical task is to establish the boundaries of the text. The possibility of connecting Psalm 18 to the previous or subsequent psalm needs no discussion since Psalm 18 comprises a self-contained unit. Three basic questions remain: (1) how does the psalm open? (2) how is it closed? and (3) is Psalm 18 one poem? Verse 1 clearly functions as an introduction with loose connections to poem itself: a third-person description of the circumstances regarding the poem's origin occurs nowhere else in the psalm. The heading is connected to the body of the poem by means of a *waw* conversive. ויאמר (an example of anacrusis) may be connected either with the end of the heading or the beginning of the poem, and it forms a hinge connecting the two. The poem proper then begins. Verses 2 and 3 contain a surfeit of references to Yahweh which may be intended to make the introduction descriptive of Yahweh's roles throughout the psalm.[1] צור recurs in vv. 32 and 47, and מן recurs in vv. 31 and 36. The thematic links (especially 'help' and 'salvation') bear more weight, for vv. 2 and 3 contain a cluster of words and images that add coherence to the overall structure.

The concluding verse, like v. 1, does not show an integral relationship to the body of the poem. The basis for this observation is largely thematic: descriptions of Yahweh's salvation come to a close in v. 49. על־כן in v. 50 introduces praise expressed in the first person, then the psalm unexpectedly reverts to a more general expression of Yahweh's salvation. Only one substantive word (ישועות) is shared with the remainder of the poem. Verse 51 was likely added to the poem as a complement to the heading (v. 1). Since v. 51 continues the intention of the psalm, it should be maintained as a part of the poem itself with vv. 1 and 51 forming a very loose frame for the poem. Verse 1, especially, shows slight structural connection to the psalm as a whole. A stronger sense of continuity and balance may be seen between vv. 2-3 and v. 50. However, these are parallels internal to the psalm in its present form, and do not serve to open and close Psalm 18.

The unity of Psalm 18 has been challenged by a few scholars. Schmidt, for example, suggests that כי in v. 32 functioned as a binding

---

1. Kuntz, 'Psalm 18', p. 9.

between two independent poems.[1] Both views command a certain
amount of evidence. On the one hand, the shift in theme with the
rhetorical question of v. 32 provides a clear disjunction from the
previous lines. On the other hand, even though the theme has changed,
many continuous elements connect vv. 32-51 to vv. 2-31. Within its
present context, vv. 32-51 clarifies and defines the help and deliverance of Yahweh. Though each of the sections may have functioned as
a freestanding unit at some point in time, thematic and verbal interrelationships make them interdependent as they are presently
connected. The nature and function of the transition between the two
sections will be discussed below.

Artistic Structure

Psalm 18 was identified in the previous chapter as a royal psalm of
thanksgiving. The rhetorical study is based on previous form-critical
conclusions rather than repeating the work. At the conclusion of this
chapter, the issue of *Gattung* surfaces again, when Psalm 18 is discussed as a unique example of the song of thanksgiving. The emphasis
is directed toward the psalm's original expression rather than its
departure from given norms. This is analogous to the closing section
of Chapter 3, where the function of Psalm 18 was described. The
rhetorical study complements the earlier treatment of *Gattung* by discussing function from the standpoint of explicit textual features. The
previous attention to function focused upon the suggested *Sitz im
Leben.*

Strophic Arrangement
With the suggestion of a *Gattung*, the rhetorical study of Psalm 18
enters its second stage. The formal structure of Psalm 18 is first discussed with reference to strophic arrangement. Strophes are indicated
in numerous ways, and the following discussion describes the textual
clues that demarcate the strophes of Psalm 18. Although the aim of
this process is structural, at many points the signals that denote
strophes are thematic. These clues are pursued as well, so that the goal
of this investigation may be achieved as effectively as possible.
     Verse 1 has already been 'bracketed' as extraneous to the poem's

1.   Schmidt, *Psalmen*, p. 29. Others affirmed the unity of Psalm 18, for example
Oesterly, *Psalms*, p. 162.

structure. Verse 2 opens the poem with direct address to Yahweh. Since v. 3 is not direct address, the critic might be led to believe that vv. 2 and 3 are discontinuous. Although there is a minor disjunction, connectedness is shown by the continued use of the first person suffix on the nouns describing Yahweh. Verse 2 reads יהוה חזקי and v. 3 continues יהוה סלעי and so forth. Also, the broader semantic range of 'strength' tends to qualify the more specific references to Yahweh in v. 3.

At v. 4 the nouns with first-person suffixes end, and a new line of thought is begun. This identifies vv. 2 and 3 as the first strophe. However, unity with v. 3 is also shown in that the theme of dependence on Yahweh is continued in v. 4. An even closer correspondence is indicated by the continued use of the first person imperfect (v. 2: 'I love', 'I trust'; v. 3: 'I call', 'I am saved'), but the theme is discontinuous. Here is the first occasion where a specific act of Yahweh is mentioned. Verse 4 carries the effect of turning general praise into a specific account, and v. 5 may be read as a direct reference to this occasion of need and conjoined to v. 4. Still, v. 4 may be read as general praise of the type expressed in vv. 2 and 3, and this dual nature of v. 4 sets it off as a transitional set of parallel lines. The lines cannot be connected to what proceeds or what follows without qualification. The first line of v. 4 agrees with the previous context of praise. The second line agrees with the subsequent context of the need for deliverance. The final determinate factor is structural rather than thematic. The opening lines of v. 7 are parallel to v. 4:

מהלל אקרא יהוה ומן־איבי אושע 4
I call upon the LORD who is worthy of praise and I am delivered from my
enemies.

בצר־לי אקרא יהוה ואל־אלהי אשוע 7
In my distress I called upon the LORD, And I cried to my God for help.

This correspondence, viewed in the light of thematic considerations, binds the verses as part of the same strophe.

The second strophe (vv. 4-7) ends with an abrupt shift in theme and language. Verses 8-16 form the theophany; in spite of its close associations with the psalmist's troubles, it stands out as separate due to its distinct vocabulary, personification of Yahweh, narrated action, anthropomorphic language, and the absence of first- and second-person grammatical forms. Verse 16 both closes the theophany and introduces a new element with the second-person address of Yahweh. The theme of the entire theophany is stated in one terse word: אפּך. The foregoing functions as an intense description of just that, his 'anger', and the explicit mention of anger serves to close the strophe.

Verses 17-20 may be read together as a short commentary upon the theophany. The strophic arrangement beginning with v. 4 and concluding with v. 20 places the theophany within a frame of references to the person in distress. Verses 4-7 are statements regarding the depth of distress and Yahweh's hearing; vv. 8-16 elaborate on the force of Yahweh's response, vv. 17-20 offer vague descriptions of the nature of the deliverance. As this last strophe recapitulates the intent of the theophany, it is viewed from the perspective of grace rather than anger, and the third-person point of view connects it with the theophany.

The כי of v. 20 marks the end of the first commentary on the theophany and begins another. The causal clause formed by כי also connects the new idea ('he delighted in me') with the previous context. Yahweh's pleasure in the psalmist is the new theme which links v. 20 also to the discussion of righteousness to follow. Verses 21-25 form a clear unit organized around the theme of righteousness. The previous comments on the theophany described its nature, while this section seems to answer questions regarding the reason that Yahweh responded to the distress of this particular person.

Verses 26-27 have already been identified as a quatrain, and עם, which begins each line, gives the couplet its unique appearance. The two verses are marked as a separate unit by their structure, but their theme connects them to the discussion of righteousness preceding. Another shift of person also occurs here, for vv. 26-27 refer to Yahweh with second-person verbal forms. The formal arrangement and change in point of view confirm the earlier identification of vv. 21-25 as a distinct strophe. Connections between vv. 27 and 28 are implied by the use of כי to begin v. 28. Second-person references to Yahweh continue through v. 30.

Thematic associations between vv. 26-27 and vv. 30ff. are obvious, although there is some shift of emphasis. A pattern of progression appears. In v. 27, Yahweh's general character and activity is described; v. 28 brings the discussion into the realm of human intercourse; and vv. 29-30 narrow the principle of retribution to a personal application. Once again, formal structure guides us in selecting units,

for vv. 28-30 are comprised of one pair of parallel lines each, with
the first word of each pair being כי. The single strophe (vv. 26-30)
contains one of the clearest, longest sustained formal structures in the
psalm. The structure appears in the initial words of the lines:

עם־	עם־	26	With...	With...
עם־	עם־	27	With...	With...
ועינים	כי־אתה	28	For you...	And the eyes...
אלהי	כי־אתה	29	For you...	My God...
ובאלהי	כי־בך	30	Because with you...	And with my God...

Notice that the unit closes with a variation (בך).

Third-person reference to Yahweh resumes with v. 31.
Discontinuity with v. 30 is marked by several features of v. 31: it is a
three line unit where the previous verses were pairs; it begins with the
unusual האל; it expresses a hymnic mood; and it diverges from the
personal (first-person) tone of vv. 29-30. With respect to its relationship with the verses which follow, perhaps its hymnic mood provides
the most important clue. The second section of Psalm 18 has already
been described as hymnic in character, and v. 31 furnishes the appropriate hymnic introduction. The word האל is repeated in v. 33, adding
continuity to an otherwise loosely connected section. Verses 31-33
should probably be read together as an extended introduction to the
strophe. This strophe continues through v. 43, making it the longest of
the psalm. Verses 41-43 show the subjection of enemies rather than
Yahweh's strengthening, but this conquest results from Yahweh's
explicit help as catalogued in the foregoing section. Verses 31-46
exhibit few formal structures, though related by thematic elements.
Only the syntax shows a formal pattern. A 'you do this for me...'
format recurs. The switch to first-person in vv. 38-39 is only slightly
discontinuous, and carries the effect of a running narrative illustrating
Yahweh's help.

The content of v. 44 alters the theme due to the first mention of the
psalmist's sovereignty, although it is connected to the previous strophe
in theme. Some contrast presents itself as well: the total devastation
enjoyed in v. 43 disappears. In the new context there is no trace of
battle, for the enemy cowers in submission.

Verse 47 introduces the final strophe which functions as a summary
of the preceding material (e.g. צור, v. 32) and an invocation to praise.
This summary of praise concludes the psalm. Verse 51, in spite of its

unique elements (such as the compilation of the terms 'his king', 'his messiah', and 'David'), serves as a final mention of the reasons for offering praise. The study of strophes concludes with the following index of strophes:

(1)	Verses 2-3
(2)	Verses 4-7
(3)	Verses 8-16
(4)	Verses 17-20
(5)	Verses 21-25
(6)	Verses 26-30
(7)	Verses 31-43
(8)	Verses 44-46
(9)	Verses 47-51

Under the heading 'strophe' one further concern has already been mentioned. The two major sections of the poem are considered separate poems by some interpreters. Certain rhetorical features justify that claim, but even if two separate psalms are identified, the conjunction of the two poems changes their readings. They become strophes, each read within the wider context created by their juxtaposition, and the theme of deliverance establishes even closer ties. The difference between the two sections arises from the individual nuance of that deliverance. In part one, the deliverance is from personal distress, while in part two, the deliverance is explicitly during battle. Other textual features will attest to the unity of the psalm as the study progresses.

Repetitive Patterns

Beyond strophic organization, the formal structure of Psalm 18 will be analyzed within three categories: the first and largest category includes repetitive patterns of all kinds; the second category involves grammatical patterns of various sorts; and the third category involves transitional lines. The study of repetitive patterns begins with vv. 2 and 3; Gunkel notes that the accumulation of divine appellatives in the introduction to the psalm was uncharacteristic of the psalm's overall style.[1] The entire psalm is rich, however, with respect to references to Yahweh (19), and titles other than 'Yahweh' occur 12 times. To find such a plethora of divine names in a psalm of praise is not surprising, but the opening appellatives are unusual, for they carry the thematic effect of enforcing the idea of the plenitude and variety of Yahweh's

---

1. Gunkel, *Psalmen*, p. 68.

help. As noted earlier in this chapter, they also serve as descriptions of the actions of Yahweh throughout the psalm.

The psalm evidences all sorts of parallelism in patterns ranging from individual lines to an entire strophe. The statement of distress in vv. 5 and 6 provides a good example of synonymous parallelism:

5 אפפוני חבלי־מות ונחלי בליעל יבעתוני

The cords of death surrounded me; And the floods of perdition fell upon me.

6 חבלי שאול סבבוני קדמוני מוקשי מות

The cords of Sheol surrounded me. The snares of death confronted me.

The precise a b b' a' pattern (chiastic structure) occurs rarely in Psalm 18, and synonymous or antithetic parallelism occurs infrequently in the entire psalm. Consequently, lines such as in vv. 5 and 6 become the more conspicuous, for parallelism here draws the reader's attention to the most profound statement of distress in the psalm. Alliteration reinforces its distinctiveness; for example ח, ב, and ל recur in the first three lines. The verbs with the first-person suffix in these three lines sound remarkably similar, and finally, a מ occurs in an accented syllable in each of the last three words. Parallelism also occurs on a larger level in connection with vv. 4-7, which show a synonymous relationship. Reading the pattern in terms of sets of parallel lines rather than individual lines, a miniature staircase pattern is shown, a b b' a'. The restatement of the call and Yahweh's answer in vv. 4 and 7 places the statement of distress in a more positive context.

A less uniform parallel relationship appears in vv. 7 and 42, as a reading in English clearly shows. Verse 42 repeats the theme (as well as some of the language) of v. 7 negatively. The phrase 'I called to Yahweh' (v. 7) is echoed in v. 42, in which the subject and the prepositional phrase are split by the words 'and there is no deliverance'. The doubled statement of Yahweh's hearing in v. 7 becomes a twice-denied answer in v. 42. This parallel relationship proves to be a crucial one as the theme of the psalm is studied later.

The greatest concentration of lines showing overt parallel structure occurs in the theophany, and again, the general aim of such parallelism would be reinforcement of powerful or mysterious imagery. One example presents itself in v. 12:

ישת חשך סתרו סביבותיו סכתו חשכת־מים

He made darkness his hiding place around him, His booth the darkness of waters.

The chiastic a b b′ a′ structure does not really clarify the image; rather, in restatement, its obscurity becomes prominent. Yahweh dwells in the realm of darkness, and to interpret this statement in terms of swirling stormclouds actually adds little understanding to the language of the lines themselves. A second example appears in v. 15:

וישלח חציו ויפיצם וברקים רב ויהמם

And he sent his arrows and scattered them, And many flashes of lightning and he confused them.

These lines reveal an a b a′ b′ pattern. 'Arrows' functions as a metonym, and only with the second line does the reader gain the key to its meaning. The relationship between war imagery and Yahweh's help becomes more explicit as the larger contexts of the psalm are explored. A final example from the theophany appears in v. 17:

ישלח ממרום יקחני ימשני ממים רבים

He sent from on high. He took me. He drew me out of many waters.

As with the previous example, a pattern of progression constitutes the parallel structure. In this case, semantic progression without any verbal repetition builds the pattern a b b′ c. The report advances from the obscure 'sending' to the act of 'taking' to the specific purpose of 'drawing out'.

Verses 26-27 contain the most nearly perfect parallel lines in the psalm:

עם־חסיד תתחסד עם־גבר תמים תתמם
עם־נבר תתברר ועם־עקש תתפתל

26 With the kind you show yourself kind.
   With the perfect person you show yourself perfect.
27 With the pure you show yourself pure.
   And with the perverse you show yourself perverse.

The first three lines are exactly parallel (omitting גבר as an addition), and פתל may have been employed in the fourth line only because the verb עקש has no *hithpael*.[1] The pattern of positive statements is broken by the final line. Formally, the parallelism is complete, and semantically, the last line provides the antithesis. The semantic pattern may be illustrated a a′ a″ b, with the threefold repetition giving a sense of starkness and abruptness to the final member.

1. Briggs and Briggs, *Psalms*, p. 157.

One final parallel pattern is noted. Verses 21-25 form an envelope structure (or staircase parallelism), and again, the structure occurs on the level of complete verses rather than individual lines. An outline of the strophe shows an a b c b′ a′ pattern with the most specific statement of righteousness in the central verse (v. 23). More general claims (vv. 21 and 25) frame this verse, and the closest parallel relationship shows itself in the bracketing lines (vv. 21 and 25). The occurrence of this structure at the mid-point of the psalm sets it off as a structural key to the understanding of its combined themes. The strophe is presented in a staircase format below:

יגמלני יהוה כצדקי כבר ידי ישיב לי
כי־שמרתי דרכי יהיה ולא־רשעתי מאלהי
כי כל־משפטיו לנגדי וחקתיו לא־אסיר מני
ואהי תמים עמו ואשתמר מעוני
וישב־יהוה לי כצדקי כבר ידי לנגד עיניו

21 The LORD rewarded me according to my righteousness.
   According to the cleanness of my hands he requited me.
22 For I have kept the ways of the LORD,
   And I have not wickedly withdrawn from my God.
23 For all his judgments are before me,
   And I have not turned his statutes aside from me.
24 I have been perfect toward him,
   And I have kept myself from my iniquity.
25 The LORD returned to me according to my righteouness—
   According to the cleanness of my hands before his eyes.

The repetition of certain words in Psalm 18 bears mentioning. The word צור performs as a keyword (*Leitwort*) which provides unity for the psalm, and at each occurrence (vv. 3, 32, and 47) it is a divine title.[1] The word appears in three hymnic statements. They are transitional statements at transitional points which indicates its importance as a keyword. The unity of Psalm 18, however, is not the kind of organic unity that can be summed up in a single word. I will propose that several key lines form the skeleton that supports the psalm, and such a theme may be expressible in a sentence, in which a word like צור would play a minor role. Similar keywords include שוע, מפלט, מגן, ישע, and רום.

Various examples of alliteration could be cited: וירכב על־כרוב in v. 11, sibilants and *tavs* in v. 12, *šureqs* in v. 47, and *mems* in v. 49.

1. Kuntz, 'Psalm 18', pp. 20-21.

Only the last two verses in this list play an important role in the structure of the psalm, and the consonance and assonance displayed in them cannot be considered a major structuring device.

Grammatical Patterns and Transitional Lines

The use of person as a structuring device evades categorization. First-person verbal forms occur throughout the poem, with the exception of the theophany. Yahweh is addressed at times directly, and at other times he is referred to with third-person forms. This interchange of person leaves the impression that the poem is, in several places, addressed to Yahweh. In other places, the narrative voice addresses an unknown third party. Little distinction, it appears, was made between these two audiences.

The use of tense in Psalm 18 is equally perplexing. Perowne offers these comments:

> The constant interchange of the preterites [perfects] and futures (so called) [imperfects] in this Psalm is remarkable, and in many cases very perplexing... Sometimes... the future [sic] must be taken as an imperfect or aorist, the time being, in fact, conditioned by the preterite preceding.[1]

Driver gives an explanation:

> Poetry... usually prefers the imperfect as the means of presenting the livelier image: not, of course that the imperfect ever 'stands for' the perfect, or assumes its meaning (!), but the poet takes the opportunity thus offered of conferring brilliancy and variety upon his description, the legitimate signification of the tense chosen... being always distinctly traceable.[2]

So, for example, when in the parallel structure found in vv. 5 and 6 the verb forms change from imperfect to perfect, the sense of the passage has changed. It might be characterized as a tone of finality. Driver's explanation, though helpful, oversimplifies the issue. Cases exist in which the imperfect would seem to make an expected, 'livelier image', but the perfect occurs instead. The major effect of the overuse of the imperfect is to create a 'running narrative', so that these past events may be relived.

The last of the formal patterns to be noted here are transitions. At

1. Perowne, *Psalms*, p. 218.
2. S.R. Driver, *A Treatise on the Use of the Tenses in Hebrew* (Oxford: Clarendon Press, 1874), p. 107.

several junctures within Psalm 18, lines are given which possess relationships both to previous context and to subsequent context (ויאמר in
v. 2 has already been commented upon in this regard). All the transitional lines of Psalm 18 help to bind together semantic elements when
the natural connection is less than obvious. Such transitions occur in
v. 2, v. 4, v. 7, v. 18, v. 20, vv. 26-27, vv. 29-30, and v. 44. All
except v. 18 appear in places where a strophe begins or ends. The type
of unity displayed by transitional lines suits prose rather than poetry,
at least according to contemporary canons. This observation lends
weight to Alter's contention that movement in Hebrew poetry is
generally semantic rather than formal. He based the observation on his
theory that in parallelism the second line complements the thought of
the first.[1] Certainly, synonymous and antithetic parallelism as they are
commonly conceived cannot provide a basis for the comprehensive
structure of Psalm 18.

Themes

The second stage of the rhetorical study involves themes, including
movement, thematic structures, and the thematic employment of structural devices. With respect to movement, the course of events is carefully limited: the trouble develops in such a way that up to v. 7,
Yahweh has not answered (even though the answer was foretold in
v. 4). In the theophany, Yahweh answers with a swift, angry descent,
coming from above, while, by contrast, the psalmist is near drowning,
below. After Yahweh has 'drawn [him] up' (v. 17), the focus returns
to the threat from which he was delivered (vv. 18-19). The thought is
next introverted, as the subject describes his worthiness of Yahweh's
help, and the introspection is expounded in the statement of a general
principle regarding the deity's predisposition to aid the noble (vv. 26-
28). The subject's confidence increases to the point that he is able to
do the impossible with Yahweh's help, and he breaks out in praise .
(vv. 32-33). He continues by describing the specific ways that Yahweh
has strengthened him for battle, concluding in v. 43. The psalmist has
by then become sovereign over his adversaries; the text displays an
obvious progression from the depths of perdition to the royal throne.
His enemies cower before him; 'therefore' (v. 50) he praises Yahweh,
and v. 51 closes the psalm with related praise that clearly marks the

1. Alter, *Poetry*, p. 29.

poem as a tribute to Yahweh's fidelity. This movement shows the faithfulness of Yahweh through the changing fortunes of the psalmist.

Movement is further illustrated in the themes of Psalm 18. Earlier, the word 'theme' referred to semantics in distinction to formal arrangement; it still carries that connotation but will, from this point on, designate larger elements within a broad semantic range. Five themes will be isolated. First, fire and water play a major part in the theophany. Second, light and darkness are complementary to fire and water images in Psalm 18. Third, imagery connected with hands relates to the discussion of righteousness. Fourth, imagery related to feet occurs when Yahweh prepares the psalmist for battle. Fifth, spatial imagery, especially associated with height and depth, provides a primary semantic range for all the psalm's images.

The phrase 'floods of perdition' (v. 5) conforms to the theophanic language of vv. 8-16. In the theophany, images of water and fire combine into a mysterious amalgam. Yahweh burns, smoke and fire descend from his face to ignite coals; yet his covering is 'the darkness of waters'. These conflicting images probably originated in the phenomena of the thunderstorm in which water (rain) and fire (lightning) are mixed. But the imagery relating to water goes beyond the rainstorm as Yahweh parts the seas, and draws the psalmist out from the deadly waters (vv. 5 and 17). The themes of light and darkness are combined with the fire and water imagery of the theophany, for the waters surrounding Yahweh are 'darkness', and his lightnings are 'brightness'. In a much tamer gesture, he 'lights the lamp' (v. 27) of his devotee.

Hands are referred to in v. 21 and its parallel, v. 25, and in both cases the reference is clearly symbolic. The word pair 'clean hands' constitutes moral purity. Yahweh supports the psalmist with his 'right hand' (v. 36), in what is most likely an unrelated action.

Except for the image of Yahweh's stance on a storm cloud, the word 'feet' is used only in connection with battle. Yahweh makes the psalmist's feet like hinds' feet, so that he can reach strategic summits (v. 34). Yahweh also lengthens his stride and strengthens his ankles, so that he can pursue his foes to the end (vv. 37-38), and after he has caught them, they fall beneath his 'feet' (v. 39). Imagery relating to feet within Psalm 18 shows direct relationships to prowess and conquest.

Certain connections exist between the use of imagery related to feet and the themes of height and depth. The psalmist stands above his enemies on the heights before putting them under his feet, an image which is carried to the extreme in v. 43 where enemies are trampled. The themes of height and depth are well established early in the psalm where, first, Yahweh is referred to as a secure height (v. 3). In contrast, the psalmist is in danger of being completely lost in the depths (vv. 5-6). These two extremes are fixed as the upper and lower limits of the psalm's spatial imagery: Yahweh himself descends from on high to draw out the sufferer (vv. 8-17); the enemies are described as haughty (self-exalted) in v. 28; and they are characterized as 'those rising' against the psalmist (vv. 40, 49), though at this point they have already been defeated and are unable to rise (v. 39). The psalmist, through the course of the poem, is submerged, drawn out, stood up, and exalted, but his enemies are haughty, defeated, trampled, and subjected. The spatial themes show two complete role reversals, during the course of which the psalmist 'ascends' to predominate over the enemies.

Function

The function of most of the artistic devices within Psalm 18 has already been noted, but two devices which are closely connected to thematic structure remain. The first is the repeated use of כי which is employed in vv. 18, 20, 22, and 23 to introduce the motivation Yahweh had for his epiphany ('because I was righteous', etc.). In the transitional line in v. 26, the word marks the end of the first commentary on the theophany. The כי of v. 22 introduces the counterpart to v. 20 ('...and he delighted in me *because*...') which introduces the reason for the reason. In vv. 28-32, the recurrence of כי adds to the cohesiveness of the longer section (vv. 18-32), for it is not used in a causal sense in vv. 28-30. The purpose is declaratory, and this may be captured by translating it 'for'. These occurrences offer praise directly related to the remainder of the psalm while the previous occurrences mark the close of the theophany.

Another repetitive structure reinforces the theme of Psalm 18. The word האל occurs three times in the poem. In each case it introduces a set of parallel lines, and these three verses are a central unifying feature. Their relationship when pulled out of context may be easily seen:

האל תמים דרכו אמרת־יהוה צרופה מגן הוא לכל החסים בו
האל המאזרני חיל ויתן תמים דרכי
האל הנותן נקמות לי וידבר עמים תחתי

31 The God, his way is perfect.
   The truth of the LORD is proven.
   He is a shield to all those who seek refuge in him.
33 The God who girds me with strength,
   And who makes my way safe.
48 The God who gives me vengeance,
   And subdues peoples under me.

These confessions stand out at important structural points within the psalm: vv. 31 and 33 form a sandwich around the verse which expresses the grandiose praise implicit in the entire psalm; vv. 31 and 33 complement the verse thematically; v. 31 closes the previous context; v. 33 summarizes the longest strophe in the entire poem; and v. 48 completes the trio by offering a summary of the conquest and subjection. The theme of the lines is narrowed and intensified in a way that mirrors the general theme of the poem.

Integrated Interpretation

The fourth and final stage of the rhetorical study focuses selectively on various key elements of the psalm. These may or may not have been commented upon previously, for the purpose of this stage is to offer a unified interpretation of the message of the psalm. The interpretation begins with a look at the way the themes of Psalm 18 are intertwined. The theophany stands out as a major thematic element; at first reading, it seems out of place in such a personal poem. The theophany is actually woven into the text of the psalm by rhetorical design, and one should notice how the theophany is framed by references to the psalmist. Verses 4-7 lead into the theophany, and vv. 17-20 close it. Both of these sections perform the function of showing the subject's direct personal interest in the theophany, and are united as the theme of a watery threat repeats itself in vv. 5 and 17. The spatial imagery continues its progression (from constriction to the 'broad place'). Though the language and action of the theophany mark it as a separate unit, it is interconnected with the psalm. All themes of threat and salvation are in this way structurally related to the theophany.

The single extensive structure noted in the previous paragraph provides a perspective from which the entire poem can be read, but there is an even more important structuring theme. This may be better named 'motif', since it occurs in a wide range of literature. Practically every image and literary device in the psalm illustrates a *reversal of fortunes*, and Yahweh himself assumes the role of a reverser of fortunes. In this connection, v. 28 may be quoted: 'For you save a humble people, but you lower the eyes of the haughty.' This unifying structure is of such importance for the psalm that its explication goes hand in hand with the following overview of the psalm's unique message.

'Salvation' serves as *Leitwort;* though Hebrew nouns from ישע occur only in vv. 36, 47, and 51, the theme of salvation occurs throughout.[1] For example, salvation stands out blatantly in the following synopsis of the themes of hearing and answering:

> He calls upon Yahweh, v. 4.
> The call is reiterated, and heard, v. 7.
> Yahweh's hearing occasions the theophany, vv. 8-16.
> Yahweh's voice thunders, v. 14.
> His rebuke trembles the earth, v. 16.
> Yahweh's answer makes the psalmist great, v. 36.
> His enemies cry out, with no answer, v. 42.
> They obey the psalmist's voice, v. 45.

The theophany plays a central role by demonstrating Yahweh's unlimited ability to answer.

A similar pattern of deliverance manifests itself in the tendency of Yahweh to make things great, large, or wide, for vv. 5 and 6 witness to claustrophobic peril. The psalmist is bound, engulfed, when Yahweh 'stretches out' the heavens in v. 10, initiating the action that results in the psalmist's presence in 'the broad place' (v. 20). He stands upon high places (lookouts, v. 34), and in general, Yahweh's answer has made him great (v. 36). His steps are broadened (v. 37) and he is 'exalted above' his enemies (v. 49); v. 51 interprets Yahweh's expansive aid in terms of '*his* [Yahweh's] king'. The psalm itself expands from the picture of the trapped individual to the presentation of a king whose domain extends to unfamiliar countries.

The theme which best addresses the key element, salvation, is the theme of strength (including power), as depicted in v. 2, the first substantial portion of the psalm where the initial characterization of

---

1. Alter, *Poetry*, p. 46.

Yahweh is '*my strength*'. Prior to Yahweh's intervention, the psalmist was obviously in the grip of overwhelming forces. He was completely under their influence, but then comes a fantastic display of Yahweh's strength. At its conclusion, Yahweh plucks the sufferer from danger. Verse 28 plays a prominent part in this thematic network, functioning as the unifying dictum. It carries the full weight of both halves of the psalm by centering their independent themes of salvation upon the righteousness of those to be saved. In this verse, רום carries obvious overtones of presumed power, עני, of weakness. These themes are applied to a larger context as vv. 30-40 portray Yahweh's strengthening in an extended discourse (explicitly in vv. 33, 36, and 40). At the conclusion of this section, the transformation is complete, so that in vv. 41-46, it is no longer Yahweh's strength but the psalmist's strength which is shown. He displays his strength in the subjection of his enemies; vv. 31, 33, and 48 have been discussed as organizing lines, since they unify the psalm due to their common emphasis upon Yahweh's strength.

Through Yahweh's strength, a complete reversal of fortunes is effected as strong enemies are subdued: the pursued becomes the pursuer. In this context, v. 18b acts as a central figure: 'They were stronger than I.' Subsequently, Yahweh's help was necessary, and praise was expressed as a reaction to his help. The enemies/foreigners are characterized as 'finished' (v. 38), 'wounded and fallen' (vv. 39, 40, 41), 'crushed' (v. 43), 'cringing' (v. 45), and 'fainting and trembling' (v. 46) after Yahweh's intervention. The reader is led to the conclusion that the enemies assumed Yahweh's seat of judgment inasmuch as they were haughty and self-exalted. The psalmist appealed to Yahweh in humility and was consequently raised to a high station. According to this perspective, Yahweh's power is supreme, and the enemies sought a power higher than their due. They attempted to place themselves in the position of the deity by determining the fate of the Yahwist, but the psalmist's close association (purity and righteousness) with the deity induced Yahweh to intervene on his behalf. As the psalm draws to a close, the subject stands on the high level (with respect to strength) of Yahweh, while the adversaries have assumed the role of complete subjection with which the psalmist began. The companion themes and related formal structures are to be read within the context of this reversal of fortunes. This does not change their function but it does determine their relative importance. Reading them in the light of this thematic structure also situates them in the progressive movement of the psalm.

Conclusion

How does this structure affect *Gattung*? Psalm 18, as noted in Chapter 3, contains several elements extraneous to the psalm of thanksgiving (for instance the theophany, the assertion of righteousness, and the preparation for battle). The thematic and formal exposition of these elements shows them to be carefully arranged, rather than artificially added. They are composed into a distinct unit with specific purpose, and form criticism would perhaps find the key to this organization in the psalm's royal identity. Rhetorical criticism shows that the unity of Psalm 18 need not bear a direct relation to the monarchy, since the unity is displayed within the psalm itself quite apart from consideration of its setting in life and worship.

In the previous chapter, two juxtaposed forms (a song of thanksgiving and a hymn) were identified in Psalm 18. The conclusion from the form-critical perspective was that the two complemented each other by first offering specific thanks and subsequently giving general acclaim for Yahweh's nature. The rhetorical-critical study has modified this view, for the form-critical conclusion was in part rejected. Yet the presence of repeated general elements of praise in vv. 31ff prevented wholesale denial, because thematically, progression from v. 2 to v. 51 was undeniable. This divergence again witnessed to the differing nuances associated with the word 'form'. The generic elements typified in form criticism led to one conclusion, but the structural forms isolated by rhetorical criticism led to another. Even if rhetorical criticism is considered a strictly supplemental approach, the wide categorization of the second section of Psalm 18 offered by form criticism must be qualified. The presence of a progressive structure based on the theme of strength, and the motif of the reversal of fortunes (as well as structural features), mark this poem as distinct. It is neither a song of thanksgiving, nor a hymn, nor is it both, since its distinctiveness sets it apart as something unspecified in any or all of those three categorizations.

Chapter 5

READER-ORIENTED STUDY

Reader-oriented approaches to biblical literature generally assume no ties with traditional approaches, except such ties as are inherent in the critic's personal method. This independent character distinguishes reader-oriented perspectives from the hybrid strategy of rhetorical criticism. George Gray claims that Lowth first recognizes that,

> Whatever else it may be, and however sharply distinguished in its worth or by its peculiarities from other literatures, the Old Testament is primarily literature, demanding the same critical examination and appreciation, alike of form and substance, as other literature.[1]

Introduction

Such an attitude opens the field for innovative treatments of biblical texts. As this introduction proceeds, it becomes clearer that the consideration of biblical material within the paradigm 'literature' places these materials within a radically different context. Criticism of biblical texts has generally been restricted to a specialized system of hermeneutics, but this alternative approach introduces textual strategies employed in fields outside of theology (especially comparative literature). This creates the possibility for many creative approaches to biblical texts.

The beginnings of reader-response theory could be traced to I.A. Richards's *Practical Criticism*[2] (1929) in which he develops a theory of emotive response; however, the 1950s are usually identified as the period in which reader strategies began. Reader-oriented theories flourished in the 1960s, and are still highly appraised among critical

---

1. Gray, *Forms of Hebrew Poetry*, p. 5.
2. I.A. Richards, *Practical Criticism* (New York: Harcourt Brace Jovanovich, 1929).

techniques. While reader strategies are not dominant within the field of biblical criticism (and show no signs of becoming so), they have exerted direct and indirect influence on much contemporary study.

Background of the Method

The plurality of reader-oriented approaches makes a general description difficult. Barbara Smith refers to a 'new stylistics'[1] which goes beyond the formal aspects of the text to consider the reader's response, which occurs through the medium of language. In biblical studies, rhetorical criticism investigates the formal aspects. While reader-oriented criticism studies many of the same formal features, the emphasis is upon the effect of the language upon the reader. Reader strategies, on the whole, have forsaken the quest for 'meaning' and have substituted the pursuit of 'effect', basically moving the focus away from New Criticism's 'text itself'. Reader-oriented critics are united by their rejection of meanings wholly inherent in the text, and this common feature serves as a minimal distinctive beyond which exist many subtleties of manner. From the standpoint of linguistics, Searle claims that whereas a speaker 'means something', the sounds or marks he or she makes 'have meaning'.[2] The difference between the two marks the difference between author- (or text-) and reader-orientations, for what the psalm writer meant is an unanswerable though intriguing question, but the question of what the psalm means to a given reader can be addressed with more positive results.

Reader-oriented criticism is not without its critics, especially in theological circles. With regard to the study of the style of a book apart from the consideration of an author, Koch claims that 'the complete individuality of a literary work, which it presupposes, does not exist [in the Bible]'.[3] Wellek responds to Richards's early approach by calling it 'absurd' that a poem should be located in the mind of the reader. Certainly, following Wellek's approach, granting priority to the reader would cause the disappearance of the highly valued 'objective

---

1. B.H. Smith, *On the Margins of Discourse: The Relation of Literature to Language* (Chicago: University of Chicago Press, 1978), p. 160.

2. J.R. Searle, *Speech Acts: An Essay in the Philosophy of Language* (Cambridge: Cambridge University Press, 1969), p. 42.

3. Koch, *Growth of the Biblical Tradition*, p. 16.

text',[1] and along with it, the single ideal reading of that text. These critiques are indicative of two major positions which stand against reader strategies. The first analyzes texts in terms of the intentions of their authors, and prohibits the consideration of texts with multiple authors as structural unities. Ultimately the text must be fragmented into its multiple redactional layers in order to recover authors' perspectives. Such an approach can scarcely provide for explication of the Psalms, since its 'authors' remain anonymous according to the design of the literature. The second position analyzes texts in terms of their inherent meanings with the understanding that since the text exists as a single objective entity it should be interpreted according to a single standard. This approach to the text cannot account for the radically different interpretations attached to individual psalms through the course of the centuries. Reader-oriented criticism is only marginally concerned with authors and objective texts, changing the context for interpretation by shifting attention to the reading process. The reader is emphasized as the primary locus of a text's 'meanings', which are produced during readings of the text.

Reading Conventions

The question, 'What does the text say?' has become, 'What does the text *do*?' Stated more explicitly, 'What is the text *created* to do?' Authors create texts in that they write them, but in a more substantial way, the text creates itself in the reading process as each reader recreates it. Reader-oriented critics examine two things at once: the first is the process of reading itself, and the second is the unique reading afforded by an individual text. Since the text is identified with its re-creation in individual readings, consideration of the conventions involved in the reading process is essential.

Affective Stylistics

Stanley Fish's 'affective stylistics'[2] provides a well-defined example of reader-oriented criticism. Fish identifies two major concerns at the heart of his method: (1) how does the text operate on the reader? and (2) how does the reader perform in interpretation?[3] Fish's approach is

1.   Wellek and Warren, *Theory of Literature*, pp. 145-46.
2.   Fish, *Is There a Text in This Class?*
3.   Fish, *Is There a Text in This Class?*, p. 2.

quite self-conscious, since the interpreter remains fully aware that a critical strategy is being applied. Fish admits from the outset that texts can only 'say' what interpretive systems allow them to 'say',[1] consequently 'the entities that were once seen as competing for the right to constrain interpretation (text, reader, author) are now all seen to be the products of interpretation'.[2] From the standpoint of an interpretive community, each reader encounters the words of a text as an experience, with the rhetorical features of the text acquiring significance only in terms of this experience. The task of the critic is to make this experiential encounter explicit.

Fish's theory introduces several significant divergences from the rhetorical approach of the previous chapter. First, he explicates the experience of the reader rather than stylistic spatiality; secondly, he recognizes that the experience of the reader (from whatever methodological perspective) is a textual strategy in itself, for readers create meaning rather than describing it; and thirdly, he points out that each theory arises from an interpretive community with its own ideas about literature. Although these advances do not render all previous criticism invalid, they should not be underestimated, since the significance of reader-oriented methods hinges upon the recognition that previous approaches hardly accounted for such reading conventions at all.

Lyric

The genre classifications of Gunkel are among the reading conventions that theologians apply to the Hebrew Bible, but the change in context for a literary study of Psalm 18 necessitates the employment of comparative literature's wider genres. The form-critical classification may assume importance as a means for interpretation, but primarily, the psalm will be considered a lyric, defined as 'any short, non-narrative poem presenting a single speaker who expresses a state of mind or process of thought and feeling'.[3] As the term 'lyric' implies, a song-like quality is also involved, which is most appropriate for literature designed for oral performance (psalms and hymns), at times considered a subgroup of lyric.[4] The estrangement resulting from

1. Fish, *Is There a Text in This Class?*
2. Fish, *Is There a Text in This Class?*, pp. 16-17.
3. M.H. Abrams, *A Glossary of Literary Terms* (New York: Holt, Rinehart & Winston, 4th edn, 1981), p. 99.
4. R. Finnegan, *Oral Poetry: Its Nature, Significance and Social Context*

reclassification may not be so severe after all, for another of the features that identifies the lyric is its conciseness and compactness, which Alter describes in this way:

> Within a small compass, through the use of intricate and closely clustered devices of linkage and repetition, it can create the illusion of actual simultaneity, offering to the mind's eye a single panorama with multiple elements held nicely together.[1]

One could imagine that Alter were speaking particularly of Psalm 18.

Jonathan Culler in 'Poetics of the Lyric' elaborates on three important conventions related to the interpretation of lyric poetry. They are (1) persona and point of view, (2) the expectation of unity, and (3) the assumption of radical significance.[2] The first convention is involved in the reader's internalization of a poem, since according to Culler the lyric itself is impersonal. Readers, then, employ several strategies in order to make the poem personal.[3] Culler names the devices that compel the reader to build a fictional context for the utterance 'deictics',[4] and includes first- and second-person pronouns, extra-textual references and many other encoded clues under this designation. According to the second convention, the interpretation of a poem is shaped by the reader's assumption of coherence. Since the reader sees the poem as a unity, each individual aspect of the poem is read in such a way that it 'fits'.[5] According to the third convention, the reading of a text as lyric invites an assumption of its significance, and the text's themes and individual statements are read in light of this significance. As the result of an abstract reading, the significance of many poems may be read as a statement about the art of poetry itself.[6]

Linguistics and Speech Acts

A careful attention to language manifests itself in Culler's proposals, indicating the importance of linguistics for reader-oriented criticism.

(Cambridge: Cambridge University Press, 1977), p. 13.
1. Alter, *Poetry*, p. 118.
2. J. Culler, 'Poetics of the Lyric', in *Structuralist Poetics: Structuralism, Linguistics and the Study of Literature* (Ithaca, NY: Cornell University Press, 1975), pp. 164-78.
3. 'Poetics', p. 165.
4. 'Poetics', p. 166.
5. 'Poetics', pp. 170-74.
6. 'Poetics', p. 177.

I.A. Richards observes that using language rather than biography (other criteria could be substituted here) for criticism can open up new meanings the author did not see, and can limit interpretations to what language is able to signify.[1] In other words, attention to the language of texts can break interpretation free of narrow historical restraints while offering a broad restraint of its own, which may be crudely indicated in the phrase 'a text cannot "mean" what its language cannot "say"'. One could object that when dealing with texts in an ancient language (Hebrew), the English-speaking interpreter approaches documents with an alien language system; and therefore the documents can only be misunderstood. The science of linguistics, however, explores the foundations of all languages, so that languages are conceived as different ways to play the same game with the same rules.[2] Consequently, the difference between English and Hebrew is not an essential difference but a conventional one, so that speech acts (and other linguistic phenomena) may be studied in one language as well as another providing the rules (grammar, syntax, semantics) are understood. One further field of information must be added: pragmatics. This may be distinguished from semantics by describing talking as pragmatic, writing as semantic; but 'the manner of talking or writing—how to say something—belongs to pragmatics'.[3] The distinction between semantics and pragmatics underscores the importance of usage (as contrasted with meaning) in reader-oriented studies.

The more specific linguistic theory put to use in this chapter originates in J.L. Austin's theory of speech acts. John Searle states the crux of a speech act approach concisely: 'A theory of language is part of a theory of action, simply because speaking is a rule-governed form of behavior.'[4] To speak is to act. Outside of linguistic strategies, speaking is generally thought of as conveyance of information, but speech act theory approaches speaking as a performance which, like the many other operations humans perform, arises from a specific situation, and involves signs and signals which are not vocal. When speech acts of

1. I.A. Richards, 'Poetic Process and Literary Analysis', in T.A. Sebeok (ed.), *Style in Language* (New York: The Technology Press of Massachusetts Institute of Technology and John Wiley and Sons, 1960), p. 21.
2. See Searle, *Speech Acts*, p. 39.
3. T.K. Seung, *Semiotics in Thematics and Hermeneutics* (New York: Columbia University Press, 1982), pp. 53-54.
4. Searle, *Speech Acts*, p. 17.

literature are examined, such situations are *implied* by the text to be *imagined* by the reader.

Austin excludes literary texts from consideration on the basis that they were aberrations of the speech act since they occur apart from the ordinary situations of speech acts.[1] This exclusion of literary speech acts was founded upon the common distinction between literary and non-literary language which has subsequently been forsaken by the majority of linguists. Austin's denial of literary speech acts was at least half right according to contemporary linguistic theory. He was correct in identifying context as the crucial feature, but the speech acts of literature are not aberrant; their functions are identical to those of non-literary speech. Their special context calls for special consideration.

The breakdown of the literary/nonliterary dialectic plays a central role in Pratt's *Toward a Speech Act Theory of Literary Discourse.* She reacted against the criterion of 'degree of literariness' as the feature which differentiates texts. From her point of view, what differentiates texts is not literary as opposed to nonliterary language, but differing emphasis on message, author, reader, and context. Nonpoetic texts are message-oriented, while speech act criticism highlights the last three elements.[2] These elements—author, reader, context—are the aspects involved in speech events (i.e., 'speaker', 'hearer', and situation).

Speech act theory offers ample potential for the criticism of poetry due to the special use of voice in the lyric, a feature which leads to Smith's proposal that 'poetry itself, as distinct from novels and stories, traditionally represents various kinds of *spoken discourse'.*[3] Not only speech, but also action, fashions the representation of a poem, for 'the text of a poem...is...formal specifications for the physical production of certain events'.[4] The 'speech' of poetry may be conceived as specifications for the acts it envisions, so that speech events constitute the reality the poem constructs. Though this is little more than a restatement of speech act theory's central tenet, it seems especially applicable to Hebrew poetry.

The speech act approach toward literary texts applies rudimentary language principles. Speech act theory, as characterized by Fish,

---

1. Austin, *How to Do Things with Words*, p. 22.
2. Pratt, *Toward a Speech Act Theory*, pp. 73-74.
3. Smith, *Margins of Discourse*, p. 30.
4. Smith, *Margins of Discourse*, p. 31.

is a description not of the truth, but of one attempt to make it manageable, or, more properly, to make it. As an interpretation, however, it has special status, since its contents are the rules that make all other interpretations possible. That is, the fiction it embodies and therefore presupposes (it is removed from examination) is intelligibility itself. Speech Act rules do not regulate meaning, but constitute it. To put it another way, the ideology of Speech Act theory is meaning, the assumption of sense and of the possibility of its transmission.[1]

Such primary aims as 'intelligibility itself' suggest that speech act theory at least attacks the problem of interpretation at its roots, but it remains to be seen whether it will yield substantially new insights on Psalm 18.

The Text as a Network of Signals

Before the study of speech acts, preliminary investigations will be offered in description of (1) the networks of signals that guide the reader of Psalm 18 and (2) the special nature of the reading process (i.e. the relative speed, personal involvement, and so on). The first investigation begins with a study of the sequential pattern of the text akin to Fish's stylistics, after which a network of centers of emphasis will be noted. Finally, one or more central matrices which organize the reader's responses into a coherent unit bring the investigation to its conclusion.

Arrangement of the Signals

Fish's stylistics, when applied word by word, offer little sense of sequence in the first few lines of the poem. Alter suggests a similar strategy which he applies to successive parallel lines, such that the first line of a parallel pair uses an 'ordinary' term, while the second line gives a more refined or more clearly specified 'literary' term.[2] Alter illustrates his point with a line-by-line characterization of 2 Samuel 22, and specifies the semantic relations between lines according to the categories below:

1. Fish, *Is There a Text in This Class?*, pp. 243-44.
2. Alter, *Poetry*, p. 13.

synonymity
synonymity with verbatim repetition
complementarity
focusing, heightening, intensification, specification
consequentiality[1]

When a line or set of parallel lines is taken as the basic unit, a sequential reading shows more promise. Alter's categories offer some help, but they are specifically designed to illustrate the nature of parallelism. An affective reading involves the complete range of rhetorical features as illustrated in the following examples.

At the beginning of the poem proper, 'I love you, O LORD, my strength!' brings the reader instantly into the context of the poem. The reader must decide abruptly if the stance of the statement will be assumed, that is, whether the statement, for the purposes of the reading, may be his or her statement. The first-person point of view makes this mandatory. The association of confessional love with strength places the reader in a somewhat subordinate role; however, the name Yahweh has already opened up the possibility for this as well as many further relationships. Accordingly, v. 3 heaps descriptive titles upon Yahweh, and the first line, 'The LORD is my rock, my stronghold, and my deliverer', combines the qualities of love and strength. The final description, 'deliverer', especially takes the connotation of force applied for love's sake, but on this occasion, it is Yahweh who exercises the implicit love as the subordinate role of the hearer dissolves. A full analysis of the operations involved in the reading of Psalm 18 could fill volumes, and for this reason, the investigation now turns to subsequent lines.

Verses 5 and 6 may be considered a single unit, since thir chiastic structure marks them as prominent, an indication that formal structure as well as semantics determines the effect of literature upon the reader. The lines read:

> The cords of death surrounded me,
> And the floods of perdition fell upon me.
> The cords of Sheol surrounded me.
> The snares of death confronted me (Ps. 18.5-6).

The language is vague, but whatever happens in this scene occurs four times. 'Death' is familiar but the other references—floods of perdition,

---

1. *Poetry*, p. 29.

Sheol—are unfamiliar to the contemporary reader. When a writer refers to a place or event that the reader does not recognize, the latter supplies needed information by imagination, and this information is subject to later correction or expansion.[1] Fish would agree that all reading follows a similar program: inferences lead to conclusions which are modified by further inferences. While the mention of death in the first line triggers the idea of ultimate cessation, the telling continues. Successive effect is difficult to demonstrate in this case, since the intent of successive lines is to repeat. Could it be said that repetition carries a semantic effect? The compounding of distress presents a sense of complete hopelessness—'I was one, two, three, four times lost'—and the reader's creation of images ceases for the duration of the lines. The individual is compelled to create a vague space of water and death, trapped in the verbal structure of the hopeless situation.

Psalm 18 contains little verbatim repetition, which leaves the reader less time to dwell on the significance of individual lines. The reader is propelled through the accounts with little opportunity to rest from the business of 'making sense', since the character of the psalm emphasizes the telling of the accounts rather than reflective thought. A good portion of the cohesion of the poem relates to the staccato presentation of a list of happenings that have no closer serial relationship than their identification as acts of Yahweh.

Literary accounts tend to be told in series, one following another. The reader's encounter begins in Sheol, into which Yahweh descends to deliver. In the section which follows, Yahweh gives military prowess in a variety of ways. The reader's thoughts are directed more by the segments of transition between these sections than by the accounts of help or distress, and the reader's involvement is determined by interaction with such statements as, 'I love you, O LORD, my strength!' (v. 2), 'I cried to my God for help' (v. 7), 'The LORD rewarded me according to my righteousness' (v. 21), or 'I will praise you among the nations' (v. 50). Such statements seem completely innocuous outside the context of Psalm 18, because the accounts of help provide the action of the psalm. The statements of praise and trust give Psalm 18 a dynamic, affective nature, and it is more than coincidence that these affective phrases are offered from a first-person

---

1. See Smith, *Margins of Discourse*, p. 23.

perspective; they make the poem 'my' poem. This same first-person point of view distinguishes vv. 32-49 as the action of Yahweh upon 'me', by which the reader is drawn into the storyline.

Sometimes it is unclear whether the reader is operating on the text or vice versa, but this issue needs no resolution, since reader and text work conjointly. The text stands as a series of rhetorical expressions ('rhetoric' refers not to aesthetic features as such but to persuasive technique). For example, the opening of songs of thanks or praise operates as a 'hook' to ensure reader involvement. 'I love you…my strength…' invites investigation into the circumstances, causes, and expression of that love. In this respect, the role of the reader corresponds to the role of an audience; the audience surrenders its right to the floor in deference to the speaker, and the intriguing titles and circumstances of texts are 'requests for the floor'.[1] The reader exercises the option either to yield the floor or to put down the text, because in order to read, the individual necessarily yields to the directions imposed by the rhetorical features of the text. One such feature is the omniscience of the narrator.[2] Since the concept of a narrator applies specifically to narrative rather than lyric poetry, it is better here to speak of an omniscient psalmist. The psalmist's 'supernatural' awareness of causes and effects convinces the reader of his authority. The spokesperson of Psalm 18 expresses a positive, faith-oriented conviction on the motivations of Yahweh's action, so that the reader grants the speaker in the text privileged reliability. The foregoing account of the reader's affective interaction with the text has done little more than suggest some applications and sketch some of its ramifications for Psalm 18.

Clusters of Signals

The second network involves the signals that draw the reader's attention to special sections of the poem which may, like the previous description of the arrangement of signals, be understood in terms of the reader's progressive interaction with the text. Some passages assume greater importance due to the surfeit of elements that contribute to the impact of the poem. Among these, three portions are isolated: (1) the list of nouns applied to Yahweh in verse 3, (2) the theophany, and

---

1. See Pratt, *Toward a Speech Act Theory*, p. 114.
2. See M. Sternberg, *The Poetics of Biblical Narrative: Ideological Literature and the Drama of Reading* (Bloomington: Indiana University Press, 1985), p. 87.

(3) the conquest and subjection of the enemies (vv. 41-46). Verse 3 attracts attention due to the cluster of divine images. The reader connects each word in some way to his or her image of the deity, forming specific pictures in which a devotee is protected by rock, stronghold, shield, horn, and secure height. The effect is to focus acute attention upon Yahweh himself, a feature which flavors the reading of the entire poem.

The theophany focuses attention upon Yahweh in similar fashion, although in this instance the imagery is developed into a single picture of divine action. Its effect is to draw the attention of the reader by means of graphic action, during which the reader's entire horizon shakes, reacting violently to Yahweh's action. This portrayal of Yahweh's response stands out as the only extended section of non-literal language of the poem. Although the psalmist's distress was also described with nonliteral language, in this case, a lengthy description is given. The interchange between literal and nonliteral segments in Hebrew poetry is a central rhetorical feature.[1] In this example, the interconnection of segments presenting the regularly recurring themes of distress and help with the fantastic vision of the theophany attract the reader's attention. The reader is drawn forward from the introduction as well as backward from the subsequent descriptions of help to this glaring image of salvation with its dynamic characterization of Yahweh. Prior to the epiphany, Yahweh has been presented indirectly —his nature inferred from the praise of the psalmist. In his appearance, the reader experiences his power, charisma, and eagerness to save which can be conceived as the poem's center of attention.

The account of the conquest and subjection of the enemies attracts the reader's attention for a different reason: the action of the poem centers upon the speaker's oppression, brought to a climax in vv. 41-46. The reader understands that this series of events occurs as a direct result of Yahweh's intervention. In a special way, the action of the poem culminates with the defeat of the enemies. The reader, who has been led to identify with the hero, now applauds his success, but the reader rejoices with the psalmist in a more fundamental way as the case of the psalmist provides a paradigm of the reader's own severe personal distress. Full participation in the reading process calls for this assumption of the psalmist's role.

---

1. See Alter, *Poetry*, p. 17.

Unifying Matrices

The third network concerns the search for a single organizing principle. The task appears formidable, since an amazing amount of action is summed up in Psalm 18. It contains at least three segments (Sheol, theophany, and strengthening for war) which the reader must assimilate as a unit, while the complete absence of a sense of time in the psalm compounds the issue ('Forever' in v. 51 is the only reference to time.) The reader may assume that the deliverance comes after the threat, but beyond this, any of the events could have happened in any sequence and with any duration. This draws attention away from a narrated event or sequence of events as the organizing principle for the reader, but some sort of coherence must be found to unite the action. One possible approach is to read the psalm as a search for an answer; the psalmist is engaged in a search for a hearing, which he receives along with Yahweh's vindication (like Job). This would focus particular attention on the statements of righteousness (vv. 21-25). Since the theme of hearing does not form a prominent part of the psalm, a casual reader of the psalm would be unlikely to decode its message based on such subtle clues.

In the previous chapter, salvation was identified as the organizing principle, and this could be pursued from a reader's perspective as well. However, from the reader's point of view, due to identification with the speaker, thanksgiving for salvation seems a preferable point of contact. At each point in the action of the psalm, the account could be prefaced by 'I thank you for...'; the object of thanks is then expressed by the formula 'you [performed, behaved in this way]...' Although no explicit 'I thank you' is given, all the deeds of Yahweh recorded in the psalm occasion the praise offered to him, so that the praise expresses the gratitude of the speaker for specific favors. Only one example of general praise is present (vv. 26-29), but even this celebration of Yahweh's justice assumes the context of specific praise within Psalm 18. The reader is introduced to the theme of praise with the first line, and the following lines explicate the causes for the poem's praise. The reader descends to Sheol with the psalmist, provoking Yahweh's response with a flurry of theophanic wonders, each a testimony of his worthiness to receive thanks. He has executed justice for the righteous, and in a multitude of ways has strengthened the psalmist so that the psalmist prevailed over his enemies. The psalm closes with praise similar to that of its opening; the reasons for praise by then well established so that even the introductory praise takes meaning from the closing. The events which induced the praise are in one sense well in the past, but each reading of the poem brings them to life as they are experienced indirectly (although quite personally) by the reader. The reader re-enacts the events, and if the identification with the speaker is strong enough, also offers the thanks of the text anew.

The Nature of the Reading Process

Having established some of the networks by which the reader interacts with the text, some comments may be offered concerning the nature of the reading process itself. One of the marks of poetry is its indecision and various omissions of parts of sentences, forcing the reader to read slowly. In many cases in Psalm 18, virtually no continuation between lines is present, and the reader brings unity by constructing a rational relationship. When vv. 4 and 5 are conjoined, the reader must build a connection between the 'enemies' (v. 4) and the distress. Once the entire poem has been read, it is obvious the threat was a military one. Within the reading process itself, a large degree of indecision may be fostered by the search for a common context for 'enemies' and 'cords of Sheol'. The figurative language takes its meaning from the more definite reference to enemies. If enemies are difficult to associate with 'cords of death', then a broader semantic range is applied in which the threat of enemies is likened to the threat of death. Psalm 18 contains several such loosely connected sections, and as each one is read, the reader is forced to consider the context implied and broaden the scope of imagination to somehow form a view which relates each to the others.

The depth of the reader's involvement assumes various levels as the poem is read. For instance, praise expressed in the first person (vv. 2-3, 50) promotes intense involvement, while the theophany represents the opposite extreme, forcing the reader to take the role of a spectator. The reader and the psalmist look on with awe as Yahweh performs, and no interaction is possible until the theophany is finished. . Comment upon the significance of Yahweh's action occurs only after its completion. The first-person stance is resumed in vv. 17-49, in which the reader remains a spectator, though from a more involved perspective, since the events protrayed are more ordinary than transcendent. The reader is at times presented with direct statements with

'I' as the subject, but at other times, both reader and narrator are placed outside of the action to witness what Yahweh does or has done. Yahweh assumes an ambiguous role with respect to the reader, remaining for the most part distant and terrible, while the force of his 'otherness' is precisely the characteristic which proves his benevolence toward the psalmist (and the reader). The reader must resolve the conflicting images of his frightening power and personal interest (e.g., vv. 16 and 17). In v. 16 Yahweh's anger sweeps aside the sea, but in v. 17, he intimately lifts the psalmist from danger, activities representing the extremes of Yahweh's action.

The Implied Reader

Such resolutions of tension play an important part in Iser's theory of the implied reader. The sentences of a work put forward expectations which are met not by the work, but by the reader. Each sentence informs the previous one and offers new expectations.[1] Once again, the language of the theophany offers the example, and the entire account describes Yahweh's appearance. In spite of the vividness of the description, more is left unspecified than is described. Even at the conclusion of the account, Yahweh's physical appearance is not described, and the description centers on the reaction of the earth to his coming rather than his appearance. The reader must make inferences concerning his appearance based on the scant images of his breathing fire and smoke, riding the clouds, and shooting arrows, images which provide the basis for the reader's engagement in the 'world' of the text.[2] Upon a careful search, the reader may discover that the world imagined is not directly created by the words of the text, but is determined by the 'gaps' in the text in the following way: 'it is only through its inevitable omissions that a story gains its dynamism...The potential text is infinitely richer than any of its individual realizations'.[3] The text presents a vast range of possibilities, from which the reader realizes his or her own perspective, and poetry elicits a wider range of possible readings due to its indeterminate character. This indeterminacy heightens the value of personal choice as the reader 'decides' what it means. Such personal choice equals (at

1. W. Iser, *The Implied Reader: Patterns of Communication in Prose Fiction and Film* (Ithaca, NY: Cornell University Press, 1978), pp. 277-78.
2. Iser, *The Implied Reader*, p. 279.
3. Iser, *The Implied Reader*, p. 280.

least from a limited perspective) interpretation.[1] Iser recognizes what he calls the 'consistent interpretation' or '*gestalt*' which is the result of the interaction between text and reader.[2] This consistency is hammered out in the reader's involvement with the text as widely divergent perspectives congeal into a single consistent world-view (the text's) as the reader's involvement in the text climaxes. The part the reader plays in interpretation is at least equal to the part that the text plays, owing to the indeterminate aspects of the text: 'Blanks and negations increase the density of fictional texts, for the omissions and cancellations indicate that practically all the formulations of the text refer to an unformulated background'.[3] The lack of a description of Yahweh's physical appearance in Psalm 18 functions as a blank, and his conflicting stances of angry judgment and personal intervention serve as negation. These two features cannot be passed off as incidental to the text, since a good portion of the message of Psalm 18 concerns Yahweh's appearance and action.

The Text as a Series of Speech Acts

Speech act theory presents a more explicitly linguistic approach to literary texts, examining the text in terms of the assertions put forward. As might be expected, a speech act analysis can be incorporated into nearly any reader-oriented study, although the concern in this study is to pursue speech act criticism for its own sake rather than to relate it to other modes. The consideration of speech act theory contains the following procedures: first, the basic categories of speech acts, as presented by Austin, are outlined; secondly, families of speech acts are identified in Psalm 18, including Searle's characterization of families; and thirdly, Psalm 18 is discussed as a performative utterance.

Basic Categories of Speech Acts

Austin begins by distinguishing 'constative' utterances from 'performative' utterances.[4] A constative statement is a referential statement which can be typified as 'true' or 'false', but performatives do not make claims to truth. As indicated by the name itself, they are

1. Smith, *Margins of Discourse*, pp. 144-45.
2. Iser, *The Act of Reading*, p. 119.
3. Iser, *The Act of Reading*, pp. 225-26.
4. Austin, *How to Do Things with Words*, pp. 3-6.

utterances by which actions are performed. Three examples of explicit performatives occur in Psalm 18: (1) 'Blessed be my Rock' (v. 47); (2) 'Exalted be the God of my salvation' (v. 47); and (3) 'I praise you...LORD' (v. 50). Austin rejects outright the claim that such statements are true or false based on the speaker's inward attitude, for performatives may be 'deceptive' or at most 'void', but they cannot be untrue in the sense that their claims to reality are false.[1] Performatives are uttered in a context which is an integral part of the performance they constitute (the matter of context will be discussed later), as indicated in the observation that 'I praise...' means one thing in a specific worship service, another in its identity as literature, another in each private reading. The context includes non-verbal actions such as thinking or meeting societal conditions, and unless certain contextual conditions are met, the performative is null. The statement 'I praise Yahweh!' would normally be out of place when shouted in a restaurant or uttered by an atheist or spoken aloud during silent public meditation.

A performative should be capable of restatement by 'a verb in the first person singular present active indicative'.[2] 'I praise' functions as an explicit performative while simple imperatives (also passives, as in v. 47) are inexplicit performatives. Other simple statements may or may not carry performative force;[3] for example, 'The LORD is my rock' may or may not be an expression of praise, though upon close examination practically all the language of Psalm 18 involves inexplicit performatives.

Austin analyzes the usage of language according to three 'acts' performed in the process of making a statement.[4] The locutionary act is the simple use of grammar; the illocutionary act is the intention of a sentence (to praise, for instance), and the perlocutionary act is what a sentence does (its effect on the hearer).[5] The force of Austin's suggestion is that communication is not simply the conveyance of factual information but a complex series of actions which are not so different from other actions. Any human action could be described as:

1. Austin, *How to Do Things with Words*, pp. 9-11.
2. Austin, *How to Do Things with Words*, p. 62.
3. Austin, *How to Do Things with Words*, pp. 32-33.
4. Austin, *How to Do Things with Words*, p. 109.
5. As presented in S. Chatman, *Story and Discourse: Narrative Structure in Fiction and Film* (Ithaca, NY: Cornell University Press, 1978), p. 161.

(1) occurring, (2) arising from an intention, and (3) possibly entailing an effect. Austin's theory has little to do with dictionary definitions of words, but deals instead with the pragmatics of language, as mentioned at the start of this chapter.

Although Austin does not apply his speech act theory to texts, subsequent philosophers and literary critics do so. According to Searle, in the context of literature, writers 'pretend' performances, and from this perspective, in the first-person narrative of Psalm 18, the author pretends to be the character making the assertions.[1] According to a similar view, 'The writer puts out imitation speech acts, as if they were being performed by someone'.[2] Literature frees the reader from the world of real speech acts, since the speech acts of literature are not binding.[3] The reader engages in escapism or play. Others take exception to this theory of literature, maintaining that the fictive text's quasi-speech acts are real speech acts set in the realm of fiction, and that the speech acts of literature do not function differently than would the same speech elsewhere acts.[4] Pratt offers the following depiction of literary speech acts: 'The real lesson speech act theory has to offer is that *literature is a context, too*, not the absence of one'.[5] According to a medial view, 'literary artworks may be conceived of as depictions or representations, rather than instances, of natural discourse'.[6] On this view, the speech acts of literature are real, but are performed within the world of the text rather than the natural world.

Families of Speech Acts

The families of speech acts proposed by Austin are general types of illocutionary acts. Searle's categories are preferable, since the names of the groups are nearly self-explanatory:

> We find there are five general ways of using language, five general categories of illocutionary acts. We tell people how things are (Assertives), we try to get them to do things (Directives), we commit ourselves to doing

1. Searle, *Expression and Meaning*, pp. 65-70.
2. R. Ohmann, 'Speech, Literature, and the Space Between', *New Literary History* 4 (1972, 1973), p. 54.
3. Ohmann, 'Speech, Literature', p. 56.
4. For example, Pratt, *Toward a Speech Act Theory*, p. 96.
5. *Toward a Speech Act Theory*, p. 99.
6. Smith, *Margins of Discourse*, p. 8.

things (Commissives), we express our feelings and attitudes (Expressives), and we bring about changes in the world through our utterances (Declarations).[1]

The categories are not completely independent, because speech acts overlap, falling into more than one category at a time. A review of the speech acts of Psalm 18, assigning them to families, should grant an overall picture of the intention of the psalm. In the following table, the lines of the translation will be denoted according to verse number plus a–d (for individual lines which are partial verses). In addition, some possible effects of the utterance will be listed on the right.

Table 3
Speech Acts in Psalm 18

Lines	*Family*	*Effect*
Verses 2-3	Assertive/Expressive	Convince, persuade
Verses 4-18a	Assertive	Convince
Verse 18b	Assertive (Expressive)	Evoke sympathy
Verses 19-20a	Assertive	Convince
Verses 20b-21	Assertive (Expressive)	Convince
Verses 22-24	Assertive	Convince
Verses 25-37	Assertive (Expressive)	Convince
Verses 38-39	Assertive	Convince
Verses 40-41a	Assertive (Expressive)	Convince
Verses 41b-43	Assertive	Convince
Verse 44ab	Assertive (Expressive)	Convince
Verses 44c-46	Assertive	Convince
Verse 47a	Assertive/Expressive	Convince
Verse 47a-b	Declaration	Bless, exalt
Verses 48-49	Assertive (Expressive)	Convince
Verse 50	Assertive/Expressive	Convince
Verse 51	Assertive (Expressive)	Convince

Each line contains a single speech act. Verses 2 and 3 are both assertive and expressive, offering a proposition as well as an expression of praise. A part of their effect includes the implicit invitation to the reader to join the praise. Much of the remainder of the psalm is simply assertive, a string of events with the effect of convincing inasmuch as the intent is to have the reader accept the plausibility of these events. Distinction needs to be made between such a 'straight' recounting of events and those portions of the text where Yahweh's

1. Searle, *Expression and Meaning*, p. viii

intervention is depicted directly. In v. 18b, the expression of motivations for Yahweh's action is in part a profession of the psalmist's belief, hence expressive, and the statement of weakness may also evoke a unique effect—sympathy. Again in vv. 20b-21, Yahweh's motivations are addressed. Verses 25-37 may be distinguished from vv. 4-18a in that the action undertaken by Yahweh is more personally presented. For this reason, it is represented in the table as somewhat expressive, but the shades of difference are very light. In fact, an expressive tone permeates the entire poem, since the claim that Yahweh saved is implicit throughout. The expressive element becomes manifest once more in the first half of v. 47a where 'The LORD lives' is purely apologetic—a claim based on the Yahwistic attitude of the speaker. In the second half of the same line and in the following line, two declarations are offered, conferring blessing and exaltation, and differing from the other speech acts in that they are directly conferred. No convincing is necessary, for Yahweh stands blessed and exalted. The praise of v. 50 is overtly expressive, but does not confer a special nature upon Yahweh; for this reason, it is not a declaration. To be blessed implies a change, while to be praised does not necessarily affect the status of the one being praised.

Assertives play the largest role in determining the nature of Psalm 18, a feature which historical or narrative texts would display. The speech acts of Psalm 18 represent an attempt to convince the reader of the 'facts' they contain, the reader being invited to assume the truth of the occurrences the Psalm relates. When the speech acts succeed in convincing the reader of the plausibility of the events, the truth that Yahweh precipitated the deliverance may be accepted as the corollary. The text affects a role which may be expressed by the invitation, 'Listen to what happened to me...' Within the perimeter of this point of view, statements like, 'Who is God except the LORD?' or 'I praise you' derive their special significance as exclamations to Yahweh and pleas probing for collaboration from those who identify with the speaker's experience. The dual messages of the text arise from its dual identities, for the reader encounters it both as an object and as an experience.

Psalm 18 as a Performative Utterance
The preceding suggestion leads to the larger task of making some specific claims regarding the character of Psalm 18 as a unified state-

ment. To accomplish this, the speech act approach must be broadened
to accommodate some further critical conventions. Specifically, the
discussion of Psalm 18 as a performative utterance is incorporated
with discussions of poetic discourse, literal and nonliteral language,
mimetic discourse, and point of view.

In poetry, the operating principles (conventions) demand that each
image, however obscure, be related to a central image or set of
images. Understanding, then, is a result of the whole, rather than a
function of sentence structure or precise definition, and a speech act
approach is not exempt from this asumption of unity. This takes on
added importance in the case of biblical poetry, as indicated by
Sternberg, who claims that the primary feature that distinguishes
biblical poetry from narrative is the former's multiple viewpoints and
orientations.[1] Within a text of this nature, some sort of dynamic unity
must be perceived; otherwise the text would be considered inchoate or
nonsensical. For a speech act approach, one strategy (the one pursued
in what follows) is to suggest a single speech act as the organizing
principle. Since a speech act in the proper sense corresponds to a
single verb, this macro-speech act may be designated an 'extended'
speech act. Psalm 18 possesses the character of a verbal performance
of praise. The speech act expanded within the poem occurs in v. 50: 'I
praise you...LORD'. This suggestion will be substantiated as the
literary conventions are discussed.

The critical proposal above exhibits what is for some readers an
unfamiliar relationship to the poetic text, influenced by two factors.
First, reader-oriented criticism grants privilege to the reader, who
'determines' the shape of the text; the critic cannot therefore blindly
assume that subsequent readers will discover the same speech event.
Some restraint operates when the readers share similar reading conventions. Second, the language of poetry provides ample space for
readers' creativity. In the course of this study, each and all perspectives on the psalm have brought new insights. Smith comments upon
both of the factors mentioned here:

> Poetic language seems—and indeed is—richer, more 'suggestive' and
> 'evocative' than the language of natural discourse... 'The more we bring
> to the poem'—the more significance it can have for us, which is why, of
> course, subsequent readings of a poem 'reveal' more meanings.[2]

1.   Sternberg, *Poetics*, p. 72.
2.   Smith, *Margins of Discourse*, pp. 36-37.

Literary texts also exhibit a certain stability, and Riffaterre's comment applies to biblical poetry in a special way: 'It is so well built and rests upon so many intricate relationships that it is relatively impervious to change and deterioration of the linguistic code.'[1] This suggests a range of acceptable interpretations governed by the objective text; the text achieves its literariness from an interpretive community. So, readers and texts co-operate not only with respect to individual interpretations, but also with respect to the limits of plausible readings. When either text or reader is given absolute pre-eminence, an imbalanced reading results.

Poetry and Ritual
One further poetic concern that relates to the nature of Psalm 18 as a speech act involves the function of poetry: 'Poetry is the traditional means of expressing and transmitting religious experience: in myth and epic, in ritual and liturgy'.[2] The speech act perspective certainly includes such an emphasis on religious experience, but the generic classification 'lyric', as commonly conceived, excludes myth, epic, ritual, and liturgy. The hymnic language of Psalm 18 attests to its cultic origin. Some common ground between a contemporary reading and cultic poetry could be found in the nature of poetic texts; for instance, in the claim that a 'poem's language looks...like a ritual or a game'.[3] Such a 'ritual' has little in common with Israel's cultic performance. Given speech act theory's emphasis on context, the two settings (lyric and cultic hymn) are to be considered widely divergent performances of the same set of utterances, to say nothing of the various readings throughout the history of the psalm's use. The reading of Psalm 18 as lyric poetry implies that its speech acts are, at most, propositional, since contemporary readers of poetry typically consider poetic texts expressions of creativity. The cultic context for poetry considers its speech acts as, in some sense, constituting reality. Since this very attitude shaped the psalm (whether communally or individually), it demands consideration. From the reader-oriented point of view, the psalm might well be interpreted as a free-standing poetic text, but its speech acts assume additional force when related to

1. M. Riffaterre, *Semiotics of Poetry* (Bloomington: Indiana University Press, 1978), p. 21.
2. Freedman, 'Pottery, Poetry, and Prophecy', p. 92.
3. Riffaterre, *Semiotics*, p. 164.

the cultic context as well. 'I praise you...LORD' functions in two different ways when viewed from the two perspectives. A consideration of both adds significance to the explication of the speech act, and both will be considered presently in the discussion of contexts.

Literal and Nonliteral Language

Within speech act theory, metaphors are considered nonliteral language, resulting from an indirect use of language. While literal language communicates more or less directly, the reader is forced to read 'around' or 'through' nonliteral passages in quest of meaning. Since the reader presumes that an illocutionary act is literal if it could be so, the literal/nonliteral determination is based on the reader's beliefs. If the reader believes that an illocutionary statement clearly does not correspond to reality, he or she takes it to be a nonliteral statement.[1] When classifying the statements of Psalm 18 as literal or nonliteral, the previously mentioned concept of the text as representative of reality comes into play. The idea that the lyric presents unreal speech acts has already been rejected, and along with this idea the possibility of reading the text as an extended metaphor is rejected. On this view, the vehicle would be the text and the tenor would be the natural world. Contrary to this, the view of the text as representative of reality allows the text's language to stand on its own since it is made up of real speech acts. The entire poem cannot be considered nonliteral, but within the context that the psalm itself creates, certain words accept literal interpretation, others will not. Virtually all the nonliteral statements of Psalm 18 refer to Yahweh; for example, the speaker refers to Yahweh as 'my rock' (v. 3). The metaphor can be understood as a way of saying something by means of something else. The speaker says, 'God is my rock', but means 'God is my protector', and 'rock' becomes a means by which a special relationship is indicated. The speaker can use metaphor to provide understanding beyond the literal because the speaker and hearer rely on common information which enables the reader to decipher the representation. The hearer must use reason to read the implication.[2] Understanding the performative nature of the entire psalm (i.e. its identity as an extended act of

---

1. According to M. Steinmann, Jr, 'Speech-Act Theory and Writing', in M. Nystrand (ed.), *What Writers Know: The Language, Process, and Structure of Written Discourse* (New York: Academic Press, 1982), p. 304.

2. Searle, *Expression and Meaning*, pp. 30-32.

praise) aids the reader by supplying a portion of the information needed. In the theophany (vv. 14-15), the grounds of the metaphors are made clearer by the use of vehicle and tenor in successive parallel lines. In v. 14 (thunder, voice) the order is tenor, vehicle, but in v. 15 (arrows, lightning) the order is reversed. Other metaphors occur within the theophany, but the examples given will suffice as instances of speech act theory's 'indirect speech'.

With respect to the mimesis of Psalm 18, the question is, 'to what extent or in what ways does Psalm 18 represent a statement of praise?' The simplest representation would be a mere repetition of the performative statement, 'I praise', but such a representation allows the reader virtually no room to explore meaning. Such a two-word poem might be characterized as 'trite' or 'insignificant'. Directness and simplicity are not the ultimate traits sought in the identification of poetry. Riffaterre's explanation of the poem's means of representing reality approached the opposite end of the spectrum, for he maintained that 'semantic indirection' occurs in three ways: 'by displacing, distorting, or creating meaning'.[1] The effect of such indirection is that mimesis is threatened, and in Psalm 18 this phenomenon appears in several guises: (1) explicit praise is interrupted by accounts of help; (2) the point of view varies among first-, second-, and third-person speech; (3) the speaker offers, with little sense of literary context, a statement of righteousness; and (4) the appearance of Yahweh is depicted in seemingly incompatible mythic language. The message of the poem takes shape in the way the poem distorts 'mimetic codes' by offering its own structure in their place.[2] If the natural speech situation that Psalm 18 represents is an extended statement of praise, how can its structure be characterized?

Point of View

The unique speech act that Psalm 18 presents should become clearer as the matter of point of view is discussed. The assertion that Psalm 18 functions as a speech act presumes a speaker. The understanding of the speech act involves not only identifying the speaker, but also determining what the speaker is doing (with, or in addition to, the speech). Austin considers three ways that the actor, in natural speech acts, may be identified: (1) by the first person pronoun, 'I', (2) by the fact that

1. Riffaterre, *Semiotics*, p. 2.
2. *Semiotics*, p. 13.

speech is heard from his or her lips, and (3) by the inclusion of a
signature (written utterances only).[1] At first glance, only the first of
these methods seems important for a literary study, but in relation to
the third, David's name in the title could be considered a signature.
The second method becomes important when the interpreter accepts
the thesis that the speaker of the literary speech act is the reader rather
than the text or the author, so that the reader posits his or her own
intent.[2] In the act of reading, 'I praise' becomes the reader's statement, which suggests a private, or at least personal, speech act. This
fits well with the personal nature commonly associated with lyric
poems, which have been described as the private thoughts of the
author 'overheard' by the reader. The personal re-enactment of praise
corresponds closely to the idea of prayer. When the 'I' of Psalm 18 is
read with a view toward its contemporary context (lyric), the poem
takes on a heightened personal nature. On the other hand, for reasons
already discussed, when the poem is read in terms of its ancient
Israelite context, the 'I' assumes a communal nature, and the poem
functions as a cultic worship utterance.

The matter now seems much simpler than truth allows, since
Hebrew poems, as a rule, do not present a single, easily identified
persona. In the course of the psalm the 'I' changes to 'he' and 'you' as,
from varying points of view, accounts pile up, one on another. The
point of view in Psalm 18 shows that the producer of the text was
either relatively unaware of self (i.e. the role presented by the finished
text) or deliberately concealing self. Since such perspectives are
clarified in the process, identifying an implied view of the author
helps the reader to discover her or his own relationship to the text.
The concept of implied author includes much more than the persona
or voice of the text. The narrator's 'I' serves only as a speaker on
behalf of the implied author. The implied author includes the total
form of the work—each emotion and the action of all the characters.[3]
According to this theory, readers naturally 'project' a view of the
author responsible for the text. The author supposed by Psalm 18
evinces the following traits: (1) strong religious convictions, including
explicit trust in Yahweh; (2) maturity developed by a wide range of
intense experiences; (3) pride in personhood and position; (4) complete

1. Austin, *How to Do Things with Words*, pp. 60-61.
2. Pratt, *Toward a Speech Act Theory*, p. 88.
3. Booth, *The Rhetoric of Fiction*, p. 73.

lack of pity for enemies/evildoers; and (5) wisdom concerning the deity's way with humankind. As the study progresses, further comments on point of view will add to this picture of the implied author. Perhaps the most notable feature of Psalm 18 with respect to point of view is the varying perspectives of the psalmist. Fish comments on the effects perspective can be used to achieve:

> Perspective is the device by which one produces in art the same visual effects as are produced without artifice in nature. It is the manipulation of surface... to produce the illusion of depth; it is the practice of deception... to disclose the real.[1]

The first-person perspective of the poem presumes the speaker's personal involvement in the poem. At times the speaker backs away to portray events from a third-person point of view, and even at these times, the psalmist does not assume an omniscient perspective. The speech act concentrates upon the portrayal of events, and the psalmist possesses only a small amount of information which the reader does not share—the knowledge of Yahweh's reasons for extending his help. Switches to a perspective in which Yahweh is addressed with the second-person pronoun show a depth of involvement nearly equal to that of the first-person praise. These shifts in viewpoint give the reader a sense of surveying a larger context than is actually present: the psalmist looks above to Yahweh, at eye level to persons attending the speech act, and above and below simultaneously as actual events are ascribed to Yahweh, providing a richer view of the action than would be afforded by a single perspective. Adele Berlin considers biblical narratives like film: they are seen from the perspectives of a person who filters all that is seen and shoots from many different perspectives.[2] Similarly, in Psalm 18, the reader views the scenes from the angle presented by the psalmist, and the conception of the speech act of praise must be broad enough to encompass these various perspectives.

Susan Lanser describes three aspects of point of view as follows:

1. S. Fish, 'Authors-Readers: Jonson's Community of the Same', in C. Hošek and P. Parker (eds.), *Lyric Poetry: Beyond New Criticism* (Ithaca, NY: Cornell University Press, 1985), p. 135.
2. A. Berlin, 'Point of View in Biblical Narrative', in S.A. Geller, E.L. Greenstein and A. Berlin (eds.), *A Sense of Text: The Art of Language in the Study of Biblical* Literature (JQR Supplement; Winona Lake, IN: Eisenbrauns, 1983), p. 72.

[There are] three relationships that operate in the structuring of point of
view in discourse: status, the relationship between narrator and speech act;
contact, the relationship between narrator and audience; and stance, the
narrator's relation to the discourse context or 'message' or narrated
world.[1]

Departing from Lanser's further vocabulary, these three points provide an outline for the final characterization of point of view in Psalm
18. With regard to status, the speech act of Psalm 18 'belongs' to the
speaker, since it is uttered by the speaker and concerns the experience
of the speaker. The contact of the speaker with the audience is kept to
a minimum, for there is no call to praise, not one imperative, no first
person plural, and no use of the second person to refer to anyone
except Yahweh: the audience is virtually ignored. From the speaker's
perspective, there is no audience; concerning stance, the psalmist
shares an affinity with the message much like the affinity shared with
the speech acts. The emotions, content, and belief expressed belong to
the psalmist, so that the speaker is in no sense detached from the intent
of the speech act. According to these indications, although the speaker
within the text is somewhat isolated from the audience, the role
assumed by that speaker is completely reliable. The psalmist 'speaks'
with evident sincerity and seriousness (and without sarcasm or irony)
throughout the poem. As the reader performs the speech act, the voice
of the poem leads him or her into a mood of seriousness and sincerity
patterned after the speaker's.

The Text as Determined by Context

Where the reader meets the text, the question of context comes into
play. The matter of context will be pursued from four perspectives:
first, some closing comments are offered on the context of speech acts;
second, context is considered in terms of Fish's ideas concerning
reading conventions; third, the psalm's context in ancient Israel is
discussed; and fourth, the contemporary context is explored and
compared to its ancient context.

---

1. S.S. Lanser, *The Narrative Act: Point of View in Prose Fiction* (Princeton:
Princeton University Press, 1981), pp. 9, 224.

Contexts and Speech Acts

Pratt proposes that 'the real lesson speech act theory has to offer is that *literature is a context, too*'.[1] With this claim, she seeks to dispel the notion that literature contains speech without a context. A major difference does exist between the contexts of everyday discourse and literary speech, however: the contexts of literary speech acts exist only on the notice of the reader. The reader 'contextualizes' the speech acts of literature by supplying, during the reading process, their conditions and situations.[2] Reading Psalm 18 as an event rather than words reinvests the words with a portion of their situational dynamic; the written word is a relatively closed system, and the speech event is similarly radically open. Each reader invests the poem with contexts that are uniquely her or his own. The psalm, then, would run the risk of meaning almost anything when viewed from the various perspectives implied by divergent contexts.

Contexts and Reading Conventions

Before reaching such a conclusion, the matter of reading conventions deserves discussion. These conventions exercise a restraining effect, allowing only those contextualizations that are considered acceptable. Texts may be described as objective realities, context as non-objective, so that context takes on an aura of mysterious reality. Critics respond to the text from two extremes: they proclaim the text's objectiveness (New Criticism), and they employ subjective readings (reader-response). 'Context' designates the space between text and reading.[3] Seung explains this idea of context by way of a comparison. Poetry as a form of aesthetic pleasure is a contextual projection. For the ancients, poetry was a medium for training and tradition, and this context determined what was essential to poetry and what was not. The same is true of the aesthetic view of poetry. The function of poetry, according to Seung, is decided by cultural norms.[4] Contextual reading conventions determine not only what poetry is, but also how an individual poem will be contextualized. The implication for Psalm 18 appears clearly: *contrasting reading conventions constitute the text*

1. Pratt, *Toward a Speech Act Theory*, p. 99.
2. See E.C. Traugott and M.L. Pratt, *Linguistics for Students of Literature* (San Diego: Harcourt Brace Jovanovich, 1980), p. 256.
3. Seung, *Semiotics*, pp. 15-16.
4. *Semiotics*, p. 118.

differently. For the Hebrews, the poetic drama was personal, centered on the recognition of Yahweh's universal purpose. The contemporary attitude toward lyric poetry differs radically. Poetry occasions reflection and at times, withdrawal, but it is not considered a world-organizing medium. In the extreme elaboration of this view, poetry fills leisurely moments as a pastime. A Hebrew poem cannot conceivably 'mean' the same thing in contemporary culture as it did for the Hebrews.

Psalm 18 in its Ancient Context

An examination of the poem in its cultic origins offers some illustration. One of the features of the text that most critics hesitate to accept as original is the title. Perhaps the 'I' of the poem became David's voice for the ancient hearer. In spite of other discrepancies between the poetic text and the title, some audience did indeed read the poem as David's speech, for this view is reflected in the title itself. Perhaps the performance of Psalm 18 reinforced the worshipper's feelings of identity with Yahweh by re-enacting the history of David. The possibility must be allowed that the Davidic background of Psalm 18 was merely a manufactured context for the song, added to insure its reading, but what the interpreter cannot say is that the poem was *not* read as David's psalm. This least important portion of the poem from the contemporary textual critic's viewpoint was likely the most important portion to the worshipping Israelite. In certain religious contexts, it would still be an important point of orientation for the reader.

Literature functioned differently for the Hebrews, in that biblical literature imposes the supernatural upon historiography; in the world-view of the Hebrews, their God was the force behind both.[1] Psalm 18 manifests a special relationship to the events which occasioned it by presenting a certain judgment of past action. The entire text offers the proposal, 'this is what happened and this is what it means'. This hermeneutic of understanding lies beneath the actual accounts of the psalm, functioning as a subtext; in spite of appearances, the psalm does not simply relate occurrences, but interprets them as signs of Yahweh's worthiness of praise. Some efficacy was found in the telling and retelling of such events; for example, Exod. 10.2 (an encouragement to tell the event of the release of the Hebrews from Egypt) is

---

1. Sternberg, *Poetics*, p. 82.

evidence that gratitude for Yahweh's acts was shown in part by telling the events to later generations.[1] Psalm 18 functions as such a retelling of Yahweh's fantastic intervention. Praise and thanks in poetry are both acts and public reports: 'here is something that happened, happens, is happening'.

The ancient context for Hebrew poetry was oral performance, which makes the speech act approach especially applicable. Hebrew poetry was composed, transmitted, and performed orally, and the context necessarily played a central role in the poem's development. There were originally very few written texts, if any; rather, the performance shaped the text. It lived in the mind of the hearer, and only by analogy can popular 'reading' conventions be imagined; 'heard' texts evoke completely different reactions than 'read' texts.

Actually, the word 'text' does not adequately characterize a Hebrew poem like Psalm 18. The full range of its effect is better accounted for by the word 'ritual'. The main function of the hymn is to offer praise, but participants are also benefited by its performance.[2] Gunkel's characterization of early worship offers some more explicit claims:

> From time immemorial Israel's worship consisted of a vast number of ritual acts which one performed for God or in God's name. Such acts, however, were generally accompanied by sacred words which elucidated them and, at the same time, reinforced their power.[3]

Ritual plays a prominent role in the psalms. Wade Wheelock describes the way rituals were enacted: 'The first person of the ritual text comes to life as the "I" or "we" of the participants who speak the liturgy... who then proceed to fashion around themselves a whole world made of language'.[4] This suggests an explanation for the absence of references to the audience of Psalm 18: the audience was engaged in performance with no passive listeners to address. Wheelock identifies as performative acts all words pronounced in a ritual with an intent to make a transformation.[5] According to an explication of Psalm 18 as ritual, the participants engaged in the utterance of praise in the belief that (in some way) their lives would be improved, and the statements

1. Sternberg, *Poetics*, p. 116.
2. Gunkel, *Psalms*, p. 13.
3. Gunkel, *Psalms*, pp. 5-6.
4. W.T. Wheelock, 'The Problem of Ritual Language: From Information to Situation', *JAR* 50 (1982), p. 65.
5. 'Problem of Ritual Language', p. 61.

involved may be classified 'performatives' to the degree that their restatement actually constituted a change in the believer's life. Although some such transformation was perceived by the worshipper, the exact nature of the change effected has been lost (due to the contrast in cultural context). Nonetheless, all poetry intended to evoke a special relationship of the believer with the deity is, in some sense, performative. By praising Yahweh with the words of Psalm 18, the devotee engages in a ritual of praise including all its benefits.

In his discussion of Hebrew poetry, Freedman notes its function relating to religious experience:

> When a miracle occurs, the causal connection between heaven and earth becomes visible and immediate, as explosive contact is made. As in any mythic or epic situation, involving the divine and the human and communication or action between heaven and earth, the appropriate language is that of poetry. Prose may be adequate to describe setting and circumstances and to sketch historical effect and residues; only poetry can convey the mystery of the miraculous and its meaning for those present. Just as the miraculous participates in history with the mundane and also transcends it, so poetry participates in language with prose but also transcends it. The miraculous action and the poetic utterance have a common source in the powerful spirit of God.
>
> We may summarize this excursus into the realm of esthetics and apologetics by affirming that poetry is the traditional means of expressing and transmitting religious experience: in myth and epic, in ritual and liturgy.[1]

The Hebrew poem may be described as a mirror which offers to Yahweh a reflection of himself. His power, kindness, justice, or even his detachment, serve as its themes. The Hebrew poet could compose nothing grander than a depiction of Yahweh's glory, and the utterances included in the composition performs many functions. One of the foremost of these functions involves the maintenance of a strong sense of relationship to Yahweh, expressed in the praise of Psalm 18.

Relationship of the Cultic Context to a Contemporary Reading

Contemporary readers of lyric follow extremely different reading conventions including the placement of much value in texts that are new, innovative, or unusual. Ritual telling and retelling are basically unrecognized as proper contexts for lyric poetry; worship conventions

---

1. Freedman, 'Pottery, Poetry, and Prophecy', p. 92.

are a partial exception to this, but they are part of a special context, to be considered later. The Psalms show a greater dependence on the 'conventional' than on fanciful design, a feature related to their communal functions. Readers of lyric who turn to the Psalms may read them from opposing orientations which are unsympathetic to their original communal intentions. Within the mainstream of poetic texts, the Psalms exert a distinctive archaic attraction, and as a result may be read as innovative texts, since their forms contrast with presently accepted norms. This alternative perspective on the Psalms cannot be considered invalid as long as it meets accepted standards for interpretation, though it could be described as a partial, or biased, approach (even if it is intentionally so).

Contemporary readers of lyric poetry read privately, and the poem is rehearsed in the reader's thoughts rather than aloud, as a general rule, but Israel's poetic texts always functioned publicly. Silent reading was almost certainly not a part of the Hebrews' repertoire of reading skills. Texts were preserved as an aid to public performance, rather than for the benefit of individual readers. The private contemporary reading of Psalm 18 accents the personal side of its statements, where the 'I' is not the 'I' among others of the same community, but the 'I' of personal introspection. The concept of self in the contemporary context of lyric poetry is private, and the reader is one 'apart from' others, rather than one 'among' others.

Another contemporary view of the function of poetry has exercised an influence on the reading of poetry. Whether the root is found in the Protestant work ethic, or the birth of capitalism, or in earlier philosophical foundations for these, poetry has commonly been perceived as useless literature. The contemporary trend toward reading for content or information has resulted in the deprecation of lyric as superficial art. In part, this attitude is expressed toward all texts that are considered purely literary objects. This trend was one of the factors which prompted the New Critics to introduce their science of criticism, which was applied, for the most part, to lyric poetry. Recently a renewed emphasis upon lyric poetry has appeared which attempts analyses of poetic language. These analyses contain, as a central part of their program, the attempt to show that poetic language is no less significant than the language of narrative. They also maintain that poetry plays just as important a role in linguistic conventions as does science or history.[1] As a result of the de-emphasis of poetic language on the grounds that it expresses subjective emotions, contemporary readings of the Psalms have been limited, even within the context of worship. The Psalms are employed for largely devotional purposes, and function as sermonic texts only rarely (their usage as instructional texts is even rarer). In public performances, they are most often employed as spirited calls to worship. In their Hebrew context, poems were not only significant, but also formed a fundamental basis for life in the community of Yahweh. Poetic texts which may nowadays be perceived as mere sentiment actually constituted the religious dimension (a very large share) of Israelite life. The consideration of Hebrew poetry within the domain of literature provides for a rather general context, and the present Jewish and Christian contexts for Hebrew poetry extend well beyond the scope of its original contexts. Israelite hearing of poetry was specific in that the texts were employed by a unified (or relatively so) community with common religious beliefs. In the Jewish and Christian readership a wide spectrum of communities and belief systems is included, and each contextualizes the poem according to its own system. The context for lyric poetry is even broader, and complicated by the possibility that Psalms could be read with an absolute suspension of all religious beliefs.

With the exception of the previous paragraph, the nonreligious aspects of contemporary readings of lyric poetry have been accented, but the poem may be recognized as lyric within a religious context as well. The consideration of the contemporary religious context of the psalm narrows the gap between ancient and modern readings. To the degree that contemporary readers who are sympathetic with the faith assumptions of ancient Israel can understand and identify with (accept) the ancient context of the psalm, they are able to append this context to their understanding of the psalm. A twentieth-century reader could not experience *the same* realization of Psalm 18 as his or her Israelite predecessor, but the acceptance of portions of the ancient understanding of the psalm enables the worshiper to experience the poem *in a similar fashion*.

One other aspect of contemporary readings of the Psalms builds a bridge between the ancient and modern hearer. Within the context of

1. See, for example, Smith, *Margins of Discourse*; Hošek and Parker, *Lyric Poetry*; and Alter, *Poetry*.

public worship, the Psalms continue to be performed orally (devotional readings notwithstanding). The Psalms were orally composed, transmitted, and performed, and present-day worshipers can participate in the tradition of public performance. The events of Psalm 18, from this perspective, would be celebrated (in various ways) as re-creations of miraculous events.

Any employment of the Psalms is contextually determined. The royal psalms originated in the kingship ideology of the ancient Near East (a previous context for some psalmic poetry). In the context of the Psalter, they have weak ties with kingship and its ceremonies, and have been accepted as psalms in praise of Yahweh.[1] The incorporation of the Psalms in the canon of scripture has exercised considerable control over their readings, and has ensured their preservation and guaranteed their authority for subsequent readers. In Christian contexts, the Psalms are placed within the single volume containing Hebrew and Christian scriptures. The reading of the latter exercises some control over the interpretations of the Psalms; for example, references such as Ps. 18.51 take on a messianic interpretation within the Christian context.

Conclusion

The application of so many divergent contexts for the Psalms illustrates their special 'literary' nature. Finnegan deals with this aspect of literature in the following statement on adaptability:

> The first and most important point is the strikingly free-floating nature of literature, the way the same 'poem' or the same genre can play very different roles in different circumstances, and can be changed or developed or held static according to the manifold intentions of the people concerned at any one time... Literature is too flexible (and man too ready to adapt it to his needs) to be directly and closely determined by the societal forms of the culture in which it is being used. Related to social forms, and used in accordance with current social conventions, it surely is; but rigidly and directly bound by any one 'type of society' or 'social environment' it certainly is not.[2]

Culler's comments on the contextualization of poetry are similar. The features that guide the reading (persona, point of view, and so on), in

---

1. Childs, *Introduction to the Old Testament*, p. 517.
2. Finnegan, *Oral Poetry*, p. 260.

his view constrain the reader to build a world in which they function, so that the poem is extracted from its original context and put to a use (or a reading) based on its prophetic character. The reader is able to read the poem because it allows for a future.[1] The poetic text, at the same time as it guides the reader, makes space for subsequent readers to understand it from various contexts. The texts which have survived are those whose meanings are sufficiently indeterminate to allow their application to future contexts. Psalm 18 presents rich emotions with colorful imagery but forces no conclusions on its reader. With a close reading, its apparently historical allusions turn out to be pseudo-historical instead, since the events it portrays are sufficiently vague (though full of feeling) that the reader may substitute his or her own 'Sheol', enemies, or battle. These features of Psalm 18, when taken as a whole, indicate that its well-defined character arises from its general identification as a song of praise or thanks, rather than its individual statements.

Subsequent contexts for the Psalms maintain only loose connections with the original context. This is true to a lesser or greater degree, depending upon the stance of the hearer or performer. The change of context in a contemporary reading of Psalm 18 actually relocates its language in the realm of twentieth-century texts. Even the context of scripture assumes a special character by virtue of the society that reads it, and within the worshiping community the language of the Psalms is dynamically relocated through the medium of worship. A Christian reading of Psalm 18, for example, might interpret the language of kingship and subjection in terms of the church's apocalyptic, as the help and coronation performed by Yahweh upon the reader becomes the promise for a dynamic future which is also perceived in proleptic (personal or social) divine aid.

---

1.   Culler, 'Poetics', p. 166.

Chapter 6

CONCLUSION

A few comparisons and evaluations of each of the three approaches (form criticism, rhetorical criticism and reader-oriented criticism) are offered in the preceding chapters. A better perspective on their relative strengths and weaknesses may now be gained by offering some explicit characterizations of each method. To defend form criticism or rhetorical criticism as useful tools for the explication of biblical poetry is hardly necessary, so interest will center upon the characterizations of Psalm 18 yielded by each analysis. Each characterization serves as a backdrop against which the method's strengths and weaknesses are re-examined. This scheme will build progressively, based firstly on the links between form and rhetorical criticism, and secondly, on the links between rhetorical and reader-oriented criticism.

Preliminary Comparisons

No simple diagram can adequately sketch the relationships of the methods. Sternberg oversimplifies the issue when he suggests that there are only two basic methodological approaches: (1) 'source-oriented' criticism which understands texts in terms of ancient content, and (2) 'discourse-oriented' criticism which analyzes a text's own semantics and effects.[1] What Sternberg identifies is only one dialectic which, among many other issues, complicates the nature of interpretation. The question of the relationship of the present text to its earliest application plays a central role in each of the three studies included in this investigation. Sternberg's proposition that both discourse and source-oriented methods must be used in conjunction with

1. Sternberg, *Poetics*, pp. 14-15.

biblical texts remains valid,[1] but the search for a pure expression of either source-oriented or discourse-oriented criticism ends in failure. They are emphases expressed in various proportion by the several methods, rather than approaches to criticism.

Form Criticism's Cultic Perspective

The form-critical analysis yielded the conclusion that Psalm 18 is a public royal prayer perceived by all worshippers as an offering of thanks. Form criticism begins where all biblical studies should begin—with the texts as they stand written—so that to some degree, the extant literature informs history rather than vice versa. The interpreter's attention is directed to a double focus: (1) the textual forms, and (2) the cultic use of these forms. In the case of Psalm 18, the recovery of the cultic context creates problems for the critic. Form criticism's consideration of the psalm as a unity is hampered by the diverse elements of Psalm 18, since the presence of different types of materials in a psalm leads form criticism to the conclusion that the psalm is, in some sense, composite. Gunkel explains that the combination of individual poems was a common practice and could not be attributed to an individual's poetic artistry,[2] but it does not satisfy the contemporary critic to identify, for example, two halves of a poem as different. A poem identified by title as a single text evokes interest in the way its parts interconnect, and the reader does sense artistic design whether that design is attributed to an individual poet, a community, or the reader's assumption of coherence. What readers perceive demands attention. In response, the protest might be raised that, with such an observation, the critic has applied alien expectations to a mode of textual analysis that was not built to conform to those expectations. This is certainly the case, but that very protest serves to show that contemporary interpreters have, in part, exceeded the more closely defined limits of form criticism.

David Greenwood lists six limitations of form criticism:

1.   Form criticism is nearsighted in that its interests are concentrated on small blocks of biblical material.

---

1.   Sternberg, *Poetics*.
2.   Gunkel, *Psalmen*, pp. 67-68.

2. *Sitz im Leben* has been limited to a single formulation, denying the possibility for subsequent settings in the history of the text.
3. The idea of communally shaped literature lacks confirmation.
4. Form criticism is prone to lead to a loss of particularity as genre and *Sitz im Leben* are assessed.
5. It separates form and content.
6. In many cases the setting can only be conjectured, so that the crux of the interpretation is in question.[1]

These observations are not of equal importance. The claim that form criticism concentrates on small blocks of material is offset by the consideration that form criticism surveys the forms of the entire Hebrew Bible, and individual interpretations are assumed on the basis of this overview. Further, the emphasis on form within the method does not commit the fallacy of a rigid isolation from content, since 'form' has a cultic and generic connotation rather than a textual connotation. Greenwood's other points are completely descriptive of the manner in which form criticism is limited.

Mowinckel's application of form criticism to Psalm 18 is subject to three of these limitations: first, he accounts for only one *Sitz im Leben* (a royal context); secondly, he makes claims for the communal formulation of the poem which cannot be substantiated; and thirdly, he posits a setting which cannot be directly substantiated. Mowinckel's search for a *Sitz im Leben* leads him to historical conclusions not unlike those of the strictly historical studies of early Psalms scholarship. For example, according to Mowinckel's enthronement context, in Psalm 18 the speaker is the king, who speaks concerning a war and against national enemies.[2] The historical setting provided Mowinckel with a framework which determined his results, a framework which was originally only a postulate. Mowinckel also has little to offer in the explication of a psalm which, like Psalm 23, rejects a historical setting. This is not to deny the importance or validity of Mowinckel's form criticism, but the trend toward historical overstatement reinforces the claim that to identify a single ritual center for all cultic poetry is to claim too much unity for Israel's poetic forms.[3] Such

---

1. Greenwood, 'Rhetorical Criticism', pp. 418-19.
2. Mowinckel, *Psalms*, p. 29.
3. See Gerstenberger, 'Psalms', p. 197.

overstatement arises from the tendency of scholarship to oversimplify in an attempt to be clearly descriptive. The science of criticism remains uncomfortable with the diversity of the Psalms.

A certain irony is manifest in the relationship between the early intent of form criticism and its actual effect. Form criticism was developed as a means of plumbing for the cultic origins of the Psalms, but in many cases the result of its application was an increased emphasis on the exile as the formative period for the Psalms. Although form criticism's respect for the Psalms was based on their earlier forms and foundations, the present form of many psalms is contrary to those same foundations. To some degree, the form-critical approach depreciates the actual texts of the Psalms, and this feature of form criticism, as well as others, shows the need for a subsequent, supplementary approach.

In addition to the shortcomings of the method itself, an omission exists in form criticism which speech act theory makes explicit: form criticism fails to account for the *performance* of cultic ritual, while a study of the speech acts involved in the ritual provides an explicit methodology. This area was doubtless too hypothetical for the formulators of form-critical techniques. If conclusions are drawn from the most pertinent information provided by text and context, inferences concerning the actual performance of the ritual can augment a form-critical study.

In spite of its limitations, form criticism displays a continued flexibility. It has shown tremendous versatility and adaptability since its inception. It is plausible to suggest that the ability of form criticism to merge with other methods and concerns is due to the diverse angles from which one may approach *Sitz im Leben*: 'sociological, anthropological, historical, and even theological'.[1] Form criticism continues to prove its worth, especially in relation to cultic literature like the Psalms, and provides solid foundations in this investigation for the studies which follow it.

1. Gerstenberger, 'Psalms', p. 196.

Rhetorical Criticism's Formal Perspective

The rhetorical-critical analysis yielded the conclusion that Psalm 18 functions both as a song of thanksgiving and as a hymn. The most important thesis offered was based on the unique character of Psalm 18: the song celebrates Yahweh's power and willingness to deliver by applying the theme of a reversal of fortunes (expressly, the pursuer becomes the pursued). Rhetorical criticism approaches the text from a formal perspective displaying a remarkably unilateral strategy. It focuses upon the words of the text exclusively, and for this reason, its conjunction with form criticism presents no incongruity. Rhetorical criticism counters form criticism's bias toward origins with its bias toward formal arrangement.

Three weaknesses of rhetorical criticism will be examined. The first surfaces in Koch's extremely negative appraisal of the method:

> Reservations must be made against the usual method of studying stylistic details, for figures of speech do not occur regularly in the Old and New Testaments, and where they do occur they are not always of equal significance.[1]

A more positive limitation can be distilled from Koch's comments: rhetorical criticism works better on some texts than others. Each mode of criticism highlights certain genres, but with rhetorical criticism this tendency becomes a flaw. Rhetorical criticism realizes its full potential in poetic or narrative texts with poetic features like repetition, metaphor, and strophic divisions. This preference far exceeds the type of inclination which form criticism expresses toward cultic forms.

The two further limitations exhibit certain similarities. Rhetorical criticism's risk of becoming a mere catalog of the literary devices of a text has already been noted; the nature of rhetorical criticism is to yield particulars. Once the literary devices of a text have been identified, preoccupation with these features can cloud the genuine aim of biblical interpretation—textual explication. Rhetorical criticism generates information which needs to be processed within some other system. The coherence necessary for a rhetorical program may be found within the text under investigation or within a system brought by the interpreter for application to the text. The related weakness concerns the tendency of rhetorical criticism to justify its own

1. Koch, *Growth of the Biblical Tradition*, p. 15.

proposals. Again, the same problem arises in connection with all textual strategies, but with rhetorical criticism the problem threatens the validity of the method. To some extent, any method designed with particular results in mind will indeed tend to produce those results. Rhetorical criticism begins with certain assumptions: (1) that the text is a unity, (2) that the text contains clues which guide its reading, (3) that certain features are more important than others, and so forth. The rhetorical critic looks for designs and unity, and therefore finds them, the presuppositions determining the outcome. This is another instance in which rhetorical criticism must extend beyond its own theory to gain a sense of perspective.

When rhetorical criticism functions in conjunction with form criticism, its strengths outweigh its weaknesses. Form and rhetorical methods should be used in combination, contrary to the tendency to choose one or the other as the basic approach.[1] Although such a union of form and rhetorical criticism is certainly possible, the tendency toward greater specialization makes a balanced merger unlikely, and rhetorical criticism's value is not limited to its use as a corollary to form criticism. Jonathan Culler's claims for rhetoric concentrate on its promise as a tool for structuralists, for whom rhetoric could be revalued when applied as a set of formal models.[2] A previous proposal bears repeating: the recognition of rhetorical features is not interpretation; the way that rhetorical features are processed is what validates or invalidates them. Rhetorical criticism involves a complete system for textual interpretation in addition to rhetoric. Still, an association (of varying degrees) between the larger arena of rhetorical criticism and some additional discipline, such as form criticism or a reader-oriented approach, accents the value of the method.

The solitary application of rhetorical criticism remains a distinct possibility, but its promise as an adjunct method calls for greater attention. Its ability to test and refine the findings of form criticism illustrates the regulatory possibility for rhetorical criticism. When its results are compared to or added to another interpretive system, that method is tested or enriched by the alternative perspective. In spite of this, rhetorical criticism is not merely supplemental, and may itself serve as the primary approach to the text. But it is such a closely

---

1. A proposal offered by Mosca, 'Psalm 26'.
2. Culler, 'Poetics', p. 179.

focused endeavor that its discoveries require placement within a broader spectrum of textual strategies.

Reader-Oriented Criticism's Contextual Perspective

The reader-centered criticism yielded multiple conclusions as well as multiple directions for further study, providing a perspective which led to two contextual points of view. First, Psalm 18 was read as a ritual speech act performed by the community of ancient worshippers as an expression of praise which evoked a special relationship with Yahweh. The employment of the psalm in a contemporary Jewish or Christian context displayed the possibility of a partial recovery of the ancient context. Secondly, Psalm 18 was read as a lyric poem which each contemporary reader experienced by identification with the speaker. In this context the psalm invites involvement in the textual drama rather than inviting personal religious experience. Two periods in the history of the psalm have been investigated—ancient and modern. The possibility for many more remains, beginning with the psalm's formulation and leading into the future, but these two are chosen as those most germane for contemporary interpretation.

Reader-centered criticism manifests several apparent weaknesses. Four will be addressed before turning to its positive features. The first weakness is discussed by John Brenkman:

> Contemporary criticism, in the wake of Heidegger and more recently of poststructuralist and deconstructive criticism, raises an inescapable problem concerning our own reception of the art and literature of the past, namely, that there is no ground of meaning or foothold in truth on the basis of which we can with certainty extract the valid significations of a work.[1]

The reader approach explores the contexts of readings without a firm hold on history. This is another case in which the interpreter must simply offer sound suggestions based on the best information available because reader-response criticism employs much supposition and is founded upon several ideals. It requires a special level of caution and sophistication for the interpreter, since offering critiques with less than exact criteria allows much more room for error. As a result, one

---

1. J. Brenkman, 'The Concrete Utopia of Poetry: Blake's "A Poison Tree"', in Hošek and Parker (eds.), *Lyric Poetry*, p. 184.

can expect that the value of future reader-oriented studies will vary considerably in proportion to the relative precision with which the method is applied. This proposition could be resisted by the claim that the historical foundations of other orientations have never been as clear-cut as the positions demanded, but even an arbitrary standard provides a basis for the measurement of results. This weakness of reader-response criticism should be understood as an illustration of the need for qualification rather than a disparagement of the method in general.

The second weakness appears in Annabel Patterson's critique:

> A theory of 'utterance' may restore vigor to rhetorical tropes like invocation and apostrophe; but it leaves unbridged the gap between writer and poem, between strategies of self-presentation and our secret, guilty knowledge that every lyric voice had an original owner.[1]

Reader-oriented criticism can result in complete blindness toward the text's personal (or perhaps in the case of Psalm 18, social) origins. The process of writing (or composition) itself must be remembered. Although the intent of the author holds no importance for the reader-oriented critic, the choice of words, use of language, and involvement in a social system are among the factors which influence later readings. Fortunately, such reader-oriented concepts as persuasive technique, linguistic choice, and implied author may be directly or indirectly applied to the work of a text's author(s). The neglect of the author is not so much a weakness of reader-response theory as a threat of rigid misapplication of the theory.

The third weakness relates especially to the application of the reader-centered strategies to biblical texts. Many interpreters dislike the idea of a non-theological milieu for criticism, for the placing of biblical literature within a larger, secular canon of texts raises the threat of indifference toward the Bible's sacred character. This apparently superficial critique demands close attention. To the degree that a text is considered a literary object, the critic's theological stance is 'bracketed'—an intention expressed by early historical critics in biblical studies as well, but historical criticism may now be considered an 'in-house' approach, since the traditional methods rely on theological sources almost exclusively. Reader-centered biblical critics, on the

---

1. A. Patterson, 'Lyric and Society in Jonson's "Underwood"', in Hošek and Parker (eds.), *Lyric Poetry*, p. 151.

other hand, continue to draw information from theorists in the purview of literature. To gain a full perspective on the problem, a further point of view is required. The stance of each textual analysis is determined more by the viewpoint of the critic than by the sources employed; consequently, little danger exists of a loss of scriptural authority when the interpreter is a theologian. The interpretive strategies of Alter, Sternberg, and Frye stand out as literary theories applied from a theological perspective, and each of these men is recognized as competent within both fields. One could not in any way maintain that Alter or Sternberg approach biblical texts 'irreverently'. Frye, whose training and experience is predominantly in the field of comparative literature, always expresses the deepest respect for biblical literature. With regard to the application of literary principles to biblical literature by non-theologians, biblical critics should not presume a regulatory role. Such critics work within a different context, and one should treat their findings accordingly, rather than accepting or rejecting their results in wholesale fashion. Furthermore, confessional interpreters need a special awareness of their own biases.

The final weakness concerns the speech act methodology in particular. Speech act theory rejects the view that literary language is substantially different from nonliterary language, but when literary texts assume a special category in any sense, they do so on the basis of their language. How can the literary nature of a text be maintained while the language of that text exhibits no difference from the language of speech? The identification of a text's speech acts as fictive utterances brings only a partial solution. Some inconsistency is involved in the proposition that on the one hand a text acts as a representation of the natural world while on the other hand its utterances are identical to those of the natural world. Pratt rejects the Formalist model which considered literature as a deviance from ordinary speech, but in the final chapters of her work, she discussed literary works as deviations from a regular pattern of speech performance.[1] Some theory of deviance seems necessary to account for any definition of literature, for without a distinction between regular speech and literary language, the category 'literature' loses its meaning.

Many of the advantages of reader-oriented strategies have already been noted. Most of these advances can be concentrated under three

---

1. Pratt, *Toward a Speech Act Theory.*

headings: (1) reader-oriented criticism addresses a wider audience; (2) it discusses the text in terms of its own language; and (3) it allows for the reader's necessary involvement in making meaning of the text. The introduction to Alter's *Art of Biblical Poetry* includes a specific address to his general audience—all those interested in biblical poetry (religious and nonreligious, scholars and laypersons).[1] As the method continues to be applied, the cross-cultural interchange offers the possibility of constructive co-operation; certain readers will doubtless emphasize certain features of texts, and balancing correctives can ensure the utility, intelligibility, and integrity of future applications.

Kenneth Kuntz, in his discussion of the unity of Psalm 18, makes the following claim: 'This is how we perceive the text intends to be understood'.[2] The language of the text determines the authenticity of the criticism, a viewpoint which provides a more reliable basis for measuring interpretive claims than an external concern such as history. A major innovation of speech act theory is that critics can analyze the way texts 'make meaning', a significant advance beyond the study of literary shape or form, for the interpretation of texts can be offered 'from the inside out' in terms of the text's own claims and propositions.

The designation 'reader-response criticism' incorporates the strongest feature of the approach. According to Smith, ' "The reader" is conspicuously hooked into the machinery...We are now to understand that the features and deviations [are] described by way of accounting for the reader's "language induced experience".'[3] This is not so much a radical new concept as a glaring omission in some previous strategies. The newer approaches exchange manageability of texts for increased awareness of the reading process, and although the objectivity of the text fades into the background, increased understanding of the reader's role more than compensates for its diminution.

Final Comparisons of the Strategies

To some extent all interpretive strategies may be considered 'readings' of a poem (or possibilities for readings). When a critic assumes a position with which to begin, that approach to the text becomes a

---

1. Alter, *Poetry*, p. xi.
2. Kuntz, 'Psalm 18', p. 21.
3. Smith, *Margins of Discourse*, p. 160.

meta-text, and the individual poem is analyzed in terms of the ways it corresponds to this meta-text. Form criticism, for example, provides the framework for a specific group of possible readings. The framework, due to its conventional restrictions, cannot offer unlimited possibilities for readings, for the various perspectives are presupposed attitudes toward a text which limit its explication from the outset, and as such, they are basically incompatible. Each operates within its own context and may only subsequently (i.e. after the explication of the text) be related to another approach.

Due to the differing contexts for the strategies, bases for comparison are difficult to find. During the course of this study, each section yielded positive, worthwhile information on Psalm 18, demonstrating that the validity of each approach is likely determined more by the critic's ability to avoid overstatement, read incisively, and communicate effectively than by the nature of the method itself (better a poor method in the hands of a skillful interpreter than the ideal method in the hands of an arrogant or unimaginative critic). Form criticism, rhetorical criticism, and reader-oriented criticism are equal in that any one of them can be used well or applied inappropriately.

The importance of reader-oriented criticism can be indicated by the construction of a model which places each of the three approaches in perspective. As is usual for such depictions, this characterization also caricatures the methods, but will provide some sense of their relationship. Form criticism locates the center of meaning 'before' the text, and the ancient pre-written forms assume special significance. The question is, are these forms recoverable? Rhetorical criticism locates the center of meaning in the text itself (therefore 'contemporaneously' with respect to the text). The question is, to what extent are the selected features original to the text (rather than reader-created)? Reader-oriented criticism locates the center of meaning 'after' the text (in the reader's experience of its language). The question is, to what degree are its discoveries testable? Both reader-oriented criticism and form criticism are 'distanced' from the text, but each deals with information relevant to the text. Rhetorical criticism is situated in the structure of the text itself but manifests a tendency to 'retell' obvious textual features. The text is examined as a formal object within rhetorical criticism, as a cultic object within form criticism, and as a contextually determined object within reader-response criticism. The last mentioned displays the significantly broader aim of exploring the complete range of the text's contextual identities.

As stated in the previous chapter, each and all perspectives on the Psalms have brought new insights. Not only does each textual strategy bring its own intentions to the text, but each also critiques the previous one(s) and informs subsequent one(s). The strategies assume more significant proportions when viewed together (as a range of interpretations) than when each is isolated. The reader-centered approach, in particular, adds a contemporary perspective on the Psalms. The Psalter, as earlier interpreters pointed out, is not a contemporary book; however, it must be acknowledged that the present-day reader of the Psalms imposes his or her modern thoughts and feelings upon the text. This is not to deny the ancient origins of the Psalms, but rather, on the contrary, to place emphasis upon the subsequent life of the Psalms. The resilience of literary texts, as shown by their continued expansion of meaning, takes on additional significance with respect to biblical literature. The Psalter, as much as any other book of the Hebrew Bible, has displayed remarkable flexibility throughout its history. The investigations (such as those offered by speech act theory) into the nature of its changes yield information concerning the revelatory nature of the Hebrew Bible.

BIBLIOGRAPHY

Abrams, M.H., *A Glossary of Literary Terms* (New York: Holt, Rinehart & Winston, 4th edn, 1981).

Alter, R., *The Art of Biblical Poetry* (New York: Basic Books, 1985).

Anderson, B.W., 'The New Frontier of Rhetorical Criticism', in J.J. Jackson and M. Kessler (eds.), *Rhetorical Criticism: Essays in Honor of James Muilenburg* (Pittsburgh Theological Monograph Series, 1; Pittsburgh: Pickwick Press, 1974).

Anderson, B.W., *Out of the Depths* (Philadelphia: Westminster Press, 1977).

Austin, J.L., *How to Do Things with Words* (ed. J.O. Umson and M. Sbisa; Cambridge, MA: Harvard University Press, 2nd edn, 1975).

—*Philosophical Papers* (Oxford: Clarendon Press, 2nd edn, 1970).

Barr, J., 'The Bible as Literature', *BJRL* 56 (1973), pp. 10-33.

Barth, C.F., *Introduction to the Psalms* (trans. R.A. Wilson; New York: Charles Scribner's Sons, 1966).

Barton, J., 'Classifying Biblical Criticism', *JSOT* 28 (1984), pp. 19-35.

Berlin, A., *The Dynamics of Biblical Parallelism* (Bloomington: Indiana University Press, 1985).

Best, T.F. (ed.), *Hearing and Speaking the Word: Selections from the Works of James Muilenburg* (Chico, CA: Scholars Press, 1984).

Beyerlin, W. (ed.), *Near Eastern Religious Texts Relating to the Old Testament* (OTL; Philadelphia: Westminster Press, 1978).

Booth, W., *The Rhetoric of Fiction* (Chicago: University of Chicago Press, 1961).

Briggs, C.A., and E.G. Briggs, *A Critical and Exegetical Commentary on the Book of Psalms* (ICC; Edinburgh: T. & T. Clark; 3rd edn, 1901).

Brueggemann, W., 'Psalms and the Life of Faith: A Suggested Typology of Function', *JSOT* 17 (1980), pp. 3-32.

Buss, M.J., 'The Study of Forms', in J.H. Hayes (ed.), *Old Testament Form Criticism* (San Antonio, TX: Trinity University Press, 1974).

Buttenwieser, M., *The Psalms Chronologically Treated with a New Translation* (Chicago: University of Chicago Press, 1938).

Chatman, S. (ed.), *An Introduction to the Language of Poetry* (Boston: Houghton Mifflin, 1968).

—*Story and Discourse: Narrative Structure in Fiction and Film* (Ithaca, NY: Cornell University Press, 1978).

—*Approaches to Poetics* (New York: Columbia University Press, 1973).

—*Literary Style: A Symposium* (London: Oxford University Press, 1971).

Childs, B., *Introduction to the Old Testament as Scripture* (Philadelphia: Fortress Press, 1979).

Clifford, R.J., 'Rhetorical Criticism in the Exegesis of Hebrew Poetry', SBLSP 19 (1980), pp. 17-28.

Clines, D.J.A., D.M. Gunn and A.J. Hauser (eds.), *Art and Meaning: Rhetoric in Biblical Literature* (JSOTSup, 19; Sheffield: JSOT Press, 1982).

Cole, P., and J. Morgan (eds.), 'Speech Acts', in *Syntax and Semantics*, III (New York: Academic Press, 1975).

Craigie, P.C., *Psalms 1-50* (WBC, 19; Waco, TX: Word Books, 1983).

Cross, F.M., Jr, 'Studies in Ancient Yahwistic Poetry' (PhD dissertation, Johns Hopkins University, 1973).

Culler, J., 'Poetics of the Lyric', in *Structuralist Poetics: Structuralism, Linguistics and the Study of Literature* (Ithaca, NY: Cornell University Press, 1975).

Culley, R.C., *Oral Formulaic Language in the Biblical Psalms* (Toronto: University of Toronto Press, 1967).

Cumming, C.G., *The Assyrian and Hebrew Hymns of Praise* (New York: Columbia University Press, 1934).

Dahood, M., *Psalms I* (AB; Garden City, NY: Doubleday, 1966).

Davidson, A.B., *Hebrew Syntax* (Edinburgh: T. & T. Clark; 3rd edn, 1901).

Dhorme, E.P., *Choix de textes religieux assyro–babyloniens* (Paris: Lecoffre, 1907).

Driver, G.R., 'The Psalms in the Light of Babylonian Research', in D.C. Simpson (ed.), *The Psalmists* (London: Oxford University Press, 1926).

Driver, S.R., *A Treatise on the Use of the Tenses in Hebrew* (Oxford: Clarendon Press, 1874).

Duhm, B.L., *Die Psalmen* (Kurzer Hand-Kommentar zum Alten Testament, 14; Tübingen: K. Marti, 2nd edn, 1922).

Eagleton, T., *Literary Theory: An Introduction* (Minneapolis: University of Minnesota Press, 1983).

Eichhorn, J.G., *Einleitung in das Alte Testament* (Leipzig: Weidmann, 1803).

Eissfeldt, O., *The Old Testament: An Introduction* (trans. P.R. Ackroyd; New York: Harper & Row, 1965).

Engnell, I., *Studies in Divine Kingship in the Ancient Near East* (Oxford: Basil Blackwell, 1967).

Erman, A., *The Ancient Egyptians: A Sourcebook of their Writings* (trans. A.M. Blackman; New York: Harper & Row, 1966).

Finnegan, R.H., *Oral Poetry: Its Nature, Significance and Social Context* (Cambridge: Cambridge University Press, 1977).

Fish, S., *Is There a Text in This Class? The Authority of Interpretive Communities* (Cambridge, MA: Harvard University Press, 1980).

Freedman, D.N., 'Pottery, Poetry, and Prophecy: An Essay on Biblical Poetry', in J.R. Maier and V.L. Tollers (eds.), *The Bible in its Literary Milieu* (Grand Rapids: Eerdmans, 1979).

—'Prolegomena', in G.B. Gray (ed.), *The Forms of Hebrew Poetry* (New York: Ktav, 1972).

Frye, N., *Anatomy of Criticism* (Princeton: Princeton University Press, 1957).

—*The Great Code: The Bible as Literature* (New York: Harcourt Brace Jovanovich, 1982).

Geller, S.A., E.L. Greenstein and A. Berlin, *A Sense of Text: The Art of Language in the Study of Biblical Literature* (JQRSup; Winona Lake, IN: Eisenbrauns, 1983).

Geller, S.A., *Parallelism in Early Biblical Poetry* (Missoula, MT: Scholars Press, 1979).

Gerstenberger, E., 'Psalms', in J.H. Hayes (ed.), *Old Testament Form Criticism* (San Antonio, TX: Trinity University Press, 1974).

Gevirtz, S., *Patterns in the Early Poetry of Israel* (Studies in Ancient Oriental Civilization, 32; Chicago: University of Chicago Press, 1963).

Ginsberg, C.D., *Introduction to the Massoretico-Critical Edition of the Hebrew Bible* (New York: Ktav, 1966).

Gottwald, N.K., *The Hebrew Bible: A Socio-Literary Introduction* (Philadelphia: Fortress Press, 1985).

Gray, G.B., *The Forms of Hebrew Poetry* (Hoboken, NJ: Ktav, 1972).

Greenwood, D., 'Rhetorical Criticism and *Formgeschichte*: Some Methodological Considerations', *JBL*, 89 (1970), pp. 418-26.

Gunkel, H., *Die Psalmen* (Göttingen: Vandenhoeck & Ruprecht, 5th edn, 1968).

—*The Psalms: A Form Critical Introduction* (trans. T.M. Horner; Philadelphia: Fortress Press, 1967).

—*What Remains of the Old Testament and Other Essays* (New York: Macmillan, 1928).

Gunkel, H., and J. Begrich, *Einleitung in die Psalmen* (Göttingen: Vandenhoeck & Ruprecht, 1933).

Guthrie, H.H., *Israel's Sacred Songs: A Study of Dominant Themes* (New York: Seabury Press, 1966).

Haublein, E., *The Stanza* (The Critical Idiom, 38; London: Methuen, 1978).

Hauser, A.J., 'Judges 5: Parataxis in Hebrew Poetry', *JBL* 99 (1980), pp. 23-41.

Hayes, J.H. (ed.), *Old Testament Form Criticism* (San Antonio, TX: Trinity University Press, 1974).

Herder, J.G. von, *The Spirit of Hebrew Poetry* (trans. J. Marsh; Naperville, IL: Aleph Press, 1971).

Hošek, C., and P. Parker (eds.), *Lyric Poetry: Beyond New Criticism* (Ithaca, NY: Cornell University Press, 1985).

Holdcroft, D., *Words and Deeds: Problems in the Theory of Speech Acts* (Oxford: Clarendon Press, 1978).

Iser, W., *The Act of Reading: A Theory of Aesthetic Response* (Baltimore: Johns Hopkins University Press, 1978).

—*The Implied Reader: Patterns of Communication in Prose Fiction and Film* (Ithaca: Cornell University Press, 1978).

Jackson, J.J., and M. Kessler (eds.), *Rhetorical Criticism: Essays in Honor of James Muilenburg* (Pittsburgh: Pickwick Press, 1974).

Jakobson, R., 'Grammatical Parallelism in Its Russian Facet', *Language* 42 (1966), pp. 399-429.

Jellicoe, S., *The Septuagint and Modern Study* (London: Oxford University Press, 1968).

Johnson, A.R., *Sacral Kingship in Ancient Israel* (Cardiff: University of Wales Press, 1955).

Kautzsch, E., and A.E. Cowley (eds.), *Gesenius' Hebrew Grammar* (Oxford: Clarendon Press, 2nd edn, 1910).

Koch, K., *The Growth of the Biblical Tradition: The Form-Critical Method* (New York: Charles Scribner's Sons, 1969).

Kraft, C.F., *The Strophic Structure of Hebrew Poetry* (Chicago: University of Chicago Press, 1938).

Kraus, H.-J., *Psalmen* (BKAT, 15; Neukirchen–Vluyn: Des Erziehungsvereins Neukirchen, 1972).

Kugel, J.L., *The Idea of Biblical Poetry: Parallelism and its History* (New Haven: Yale University Press, 1981).

Kuntz, J.K., 'Psalm 18: A Rhetorical-Critical Analysis', *JSOT* 26 (1983), pp. 3-31.

Lanser, S.S., *The Narrative Act: Point of View in Prose Fiction* (Princeton: Princeton University Press, 1981).

Levin, S.R., 'The Conventions of Poetry', in S. Chatman (ed.), *Literary Style: A Symposium* (London: Oxford University Press, 1971).

Lowth, R., *Isaiah: A New Translation with a Preliminary Dissertation* (London: T. Cadell, 3rd edn, 1975).

—*Lectures on the Sacred Poetry of the Hebrews* (trans. G. Gregory; Boston: Crocker & Brewster, 1829).

Mosca, P.G., 'Psalm 26: Poetic Structure and the Form-Critical Task', *CBQ* 47 (1985), pp. 212-37.

Mowinckel, S., *The Psalms in Israel's Worship* (trans. D.R. Ap-Thomas; 2 vols.; Oxford: Basil Blackwell, 1962).

Muilenburg, J., 'Form Criticism and Beyond', *JBL* 88 (1960), pp. 1-18.

Oesterly, W.O.E., *The Psalms* (London: SPCK, 1953).

Ohmann, R., 'Speech, Literature, and the Space Between', *New Literary History* 4.1 (1972–73), pp. 47-63.

Perowne, J.J.S., *The Book of Psalms* (Grand Rapids: Zondervan, 1 vol. edn, 1976).

Porter, J.A., *The Drama of Speech Acts: Shakespeare's Lancastrian Tetralogy* (Berkeley: University of California Press, 1979).

Pratt, M.L., *Toward a Speech Act Theory of Literary Discourse* (Bloomington: Indiana University Press, 1977).

Pritchard, J.B. (ed.), *The Ancient Near East: An Anthology of Texts and Pictures* (Princeton: Princeton University Press, 1958).

—*The Ancient Near East Volume 2: A New Anthology of Texts and Pictures* (Princeton: Princeton University Press, 1975).

Richards, I.A., *Practical Criticism* (New York: Harcourt Brace Jovanovich, 1929).

Riffaterre, M., *Semiotics of Poetry* (Bloomington: Indiana University Press, 1978).

Roberts, B.J., *The Old Testament Text and Versions: The Hebrew Text in Transmission and the History of the Ancient Versions* (Cardiff: University of Wales Press, 1951).

Robinson, T.H., *The Poetry of the Old Testament* (London: Duckworth, 1947).

Schmidt, H., *Die Psalmen* (Tübingen: Mohr [Paul Siebeck], 1934).

Searle, J.R., *Expression and Meaning: Studies in the Theory of Speech Acts* (Cambridge: Cambridge University Press, 1979).

—*Speech Acts: An Essay in the Philosophy of Language* (Cambridge: Cambridge University Press, 1979).

Sebeok, T.A. (ed.), *Style in Language* (New York: The Technology Press of Massachusetts Institute of Technology and John Wiley & Sons, 1960).

Seung, T.K., *Semiotics in Thematics and Hermeneutics* (New York: Columbia University Press, 1982).

Smith, B.H., *On the Margins of Discourse: The Relation of Literature to Language* (Chicago: University of Chicago Press, 1978).

Smith, G.A., *The Early Poetry of Israel in Its Physical and Social Origins* (London: Oxford University Press, 1912).

Steinmann, M., Jr., 'Speech Act Theory and Writing', in M. Nystrand (ed.), *What Writers Know: The Language, Process, and Structure of Written Discourse* (New York: Academic Press, 1982).

Sternberg, M., *The Poetics of Biblical Narrative: Ideological Literature and the Drama of Reading* (Bloomington: Indiana University Press, 1985).

Stuart, D.K., *Studies in Early Hebrew Meter* (Missoula, MT: Scholars Press, 1976).

Tate, M.E., 'The Interpretation of the Psalms', *RevExp* 81 (1984), pp. 363-75.

Thomas, D.W., 'בליעל in the Old Testament', in J.N. Birdsall and R.W. Thomson (eds.), *Biblical and Patristic Studies in Memory of R.P. Casey* (New York: Herder, 1963).

Tompkins, J.P. (ed.), *Reader Response Criticism: From Formalism to Post-Structuralism* (Baltimore: Johns Hopkins University Press, 1980).

Traugott, E.C., and M.L. Pratt, *Linguistics for Students of Literature* (San Diego: Harcourt Brace Jovanovich, 1980).

Ullman, S., *Language and Style* (New York: Barnes & Noble, 1964).

Watson, W.G.E., *Classical Hebrew Poetry: A Guide to its Techniques* (JSOTSup, 26; Sheffield: JSOT Press, 1984).

Watters, W.R., *Formula Criticism and the Poetry of the Old Testament* (New York: De Gruyter, 1976).

Weingreen, J., *Introduction to the Critical Study of the Text of the Hebrew Bible* (London: Oxford University Press, 1982).

Weiser, A., *The Psalms* (OTL; Philadelphia: Westminster Press, 1962).

Wellek, R., and A. Warren, *Theory of Literature* (New York: Harcourt Brace Jovanovich, 3rd edn, 1977).

Wellhausen, J., *The Book of Psalms: Critical Edition of the Hebrew Text* (The Sacred Books of the Old Testament, 14; Baltimore: Johns Hopkins University Press, 1895).

Westermann, C., *Praise and Lament in the Psalms* (trans. K.R. Crim and R.N. Soulen; Atlanta: John Knox Press, 1981).

Wheelock, W.T., 'The Problem of Ritual Language: From Information to Situation', *JAAR* 50 (1982), pp. 49-71.

INDEXES

INDEX OF REFERENCES

OLD TESTAMENT